The Vision of His Glory

Finding Hope Through the Revelation of Jesus Christ

WORKBOOK

Anne Graham Lotz

LifeWay Press
Nashville, Tennessee

ISBN 0-7673-9116-0

Dewey Decimal Classification Number: 248.84
Subject Heading: HOPE\BIBLE. N.T. REVELATION—STUDY AND TEACHING

This book is the text for course CG-0475 in the subject area
Personal Life in the Christian Growth Study Plan.

Unless stated otherwise, the Scripture quotations in this book are from the Holy Bible,
New International Version, copyright © 1973, 1978, 1984 by International Bible Society.

For more on *The Vision of His Glory* resources, WRITE LifeWay Church Resources
Customer Service, 127 Ninth Avenue, North, Nashville, TN 37234-0113;
FAX order to (615) 251-5933; PHONE 1-800-458-2772;
EMAIL *CustomerService@lifeway.com*; order ONLINE at *www.lifeway.com;*
or visit the LifeWay Christian Store serving you.

Printed in the United States of America

✝

LifeWay Press
127 Ninth Avenue, North
Nashville, Tennessee 37234-0151

As God works through us ...
We will help people and churches know Jesus Christ and seek His Kingdom
by providing biblical solutions that spiritually transform individuals and cultures.

CONTENTS

Anne Graham Lotz

Anne, originally from Montreat, North Carolina, is the second daughter of Billy and Ruth Graham. She is the wife of Dr. Daniel M. Lotz and the mother of three married children. Having taught Bible classes for 13 years, Anne established AnGeL Ministries in 1988. Anne seeks to bring revival to the hearts of God's people with her clear, consistent message, calling them to know God in a personal relationship through His Word. Along with *The Vision of His Glory*, Anne has written *God's Story*. Both books are Gold Medallion Award winners for excellence in Bible study by the Evangelical Christian Publishers Association.

AnGeL Ministries is a non-profit organization that seeks to revive the hearts of God's people through drawing them into His Word that they might know Him.
Contact AnGeL Ministries,
P.O. Box 31167,
Raleigh, NC 27622-1167.

PREFACE

*I*s the Book of Revelation confusing to you? Although printed in black and white, translated into English, using everyday nouns, verbs and acceptable sentence structure, do you sometimes read it, thinking it must be written in some form of cryptic code? *The Vision of His Glory* will help you break the "code," so that rather than be confusing, the Book of Revelation will help you clearly communicate with the Lord Whom the book reveals.

Communication is vitally important in developing a personal relationship with anyone, including God. Could it be that lack of communication, or even miscommunication, could be one reason for your relationship with God seeming to be distant, formal, and impersonal?

Recently I was given this collection of church bulletin misprints:

➢ *The rosebud on the altar this morning is to announce the birth of David Alan Belser, the sin of Rev. and Mrs. Julius Belser.*
➢ *Altar flowers are given to the glory of God in memory of her mother.*
➢ *The message this evening will be "What Is Hell Like?" Come early and listen to the choir practice.*
➢ *The outreach committee has enlisted 25 visitors to make calls on people who are not afflicted with any church.*
➢ *Peacemaking meeting canceled for today due to a conflict.*
➢ *Ushers will eat latecomers.*
➢ *Low self-esteem support group, 7:00 to 8:30 p.m., Eastview Baptist Church (use back door).*

As humorous as these misprints are, miscommunication is not funny when we are seeking to understand God's Word. Therefore, it is important to take the time and make the effort to read His Word carefully and accurately, that we might hear His voice speaking to us personally.

The Vision of His Glory begins with a workshop on how to read and study the Bible. This approach is then used in the study of Revelation. It is my heartfelt prayer that this course will aid you in developing your communication with God and therefore your personal relationship with God. And that in the process, you might be thrilled by the vision of His glory!

Anne Graham Lotz

ABOUT THE STUDY

*T*his workbook is primarily to be used with the video course *The Vision of His Glory*, but it can also be used as a companion to the book *The Vision of His Glory*. As an integral part of the video course, it provides a format for Bible study that serves as the basis for small-group study (Bible study classes, home or neighborhood studies, one-on-one discipleship) and individual study. Believing that God speaks to us through His Word, this workbook leads you through a series of three questions. The questions enable you not only to discover for yourself the eternal truths revealed by God in the Bible, but also to hear God speaking personally through His Word. You are then prepared to participate in a meaningful small-group experience that features a video presentation by Anne Graham Lotz and discussion with other participants.

Individual Study

The course begins with a Bible study workshop. After participating in the workshop, you will be familiar with an approach to Bible study that will challenge you to hear and apply God's Word as never before. Then you will use this approach as you study Revelation.

The first section of each seminar contains Scripture for individual study in preparation for the small-group time. Several portions of Scripture are provided for each seminar.

The video presentation during the small-group time will be more meaningful if all Scripture portions are completed prior to the group meeting.

Effective daily Bible study will occur if you:

➤ *Set aside a regular place for private devotions.*

➤ *Set aside a regular time for private devotions.*

➤ *Pray before beginning the day's assignment, asking God to speak to you through His Word.*

➤ *Write out your answers for each step in sequence.*

➤ *Make the time to be still and listen, reflecting thoughtfully on your response in the final step.*

➤ *Don't rush. It may take you several days of prayerful meditation on a given passage to discover meaningful lessons and hear God speaking to you. The object is not to get through the material, but to develop your personal relationship with God.*

The separate audiotape set available with this resource can be used to support individual study. The tapes can serve as a review of the video presentations or as a way to make up a missed session.

Spiritual discipline is an essential part of a person's ability to grow in his or her personal relationship with God through knowledge and understanding of His Word.

Take your individual study seriously and allow God to speak to you from His Word.

Group Study

Group study begins with a workshop on how to study and apply God's Word. At the conclusion of the workshop, you will be instructed to complete individual study for the first seminar session.

Once a week or once a month, depending on how often your group decides to meet, participants gather to watch a video presentation by Anne Graham Lotz and share insights from their individual study. Your group may decide to view the entire video presentation each time you meet, or you may want to divide the presentation and view each seminar over two sessions. Allow 90 minutes per session if you view the entire presentation.

A viewing guide is provided for each seminar for you to take notes during the video presentation. After the presentation, your group facilitator leads participants in discussion using the Group Leader Guide on page 117. If the group is large (12 or more), the facilitator may divide the large group for discussion with moderators chosen to facilitate each small group.

The Vision of His Glory includes the Bible study workshop and six seminar sessions on Revelation. If your group uses the 90-minute session format, the course can be completed in 7 weekly sessions, 7 monthly sessions, or any schedule your group determines best for them.

The Vision of His Glory

The Book of Revelation may be difficult for you in certain passages. Don't get hung up on symbolism. Look for the general principles and lessons which can be learned, even when the symbolism is not fully understood. An example is given at the beginning of each column of the worksheets to help you get started.

Read the Book of Revelation prayerfully, objectively, thoughtfully, and attentively as you listen for God to speak. He may not speak to you through every verse, but God will speak. When He does, respond to God and grow in your personal relationship with Him.

Study Note

The video study does not cover every verse in the Book of Revelation. For example, three of the seven churches in chapters 2 and 3 are not discussed. Only portions of chapters 6–19 have been included. Chapter 20 is not addressed. For Anne's treatment of these and other passages, refer to the book *The Vision of His Glory*. You are encouraged to use the Bible study approach presented in the workshop in your personal study of these passages.

BIBLE STUDY WORKSHOP

The Bible Study Workshop has a single purpose: to present an approach that will help you know God in a personal relationship through His Word. The Bible study approach you will be introduced to will help you communicate with God through the Bible.

The following information is introduced in detail on the video presentation. Use this section as your viewing guide and workshop material. Underline key thoughts and take additional notes as you participate in the workshop.

What You Need for Bible Study

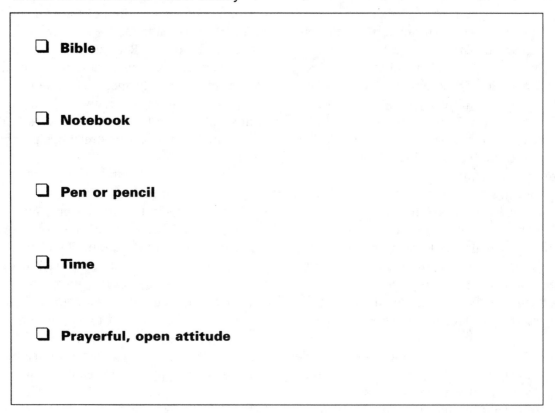

❏ **Bible**

❏ **Notebook**

❏ **Pen or pencil**

❏ **Time**

❏ **Prayerful, open attitude**

Steps to Bible Study

S T E P 1
_____

Look in God's Word.
Begin by reading the designated passage of Scripture.

S T E P 2
_____

What does the passage say?
When you have finished reading the passage, make a verse-by-verse
list of the outstanding facts. Don't get caught up in the details, just
pinpoint the most obvious facts. Ask yourself, "Who is speaking?
What is the subject? Where is it taking place? When did it happen?"
As you make your list, do not paraphrase, but use actual words
from the passage itself.

STEP 3

What does the passage mean?

After reading the passage and listing the facts, look for a lesson to learn from each fact. Ask yourself, "What are the people doing that I should be doing? Is there a command I should obey? A promise I should claim? A warning I should heed? An example I should follow?" Focus on spiritual lessons.

STEP 4

What does the passage mean to me?

The most meaningful step is step 4; but you can't do step 4 until you complete the first three steps. Take the lessons you identified in step 3 and put them in the form of a question you could ask yourself, your spouse, your child, your friend, your neighbor, or your coworker. As you write the questions, listen for God to communicate to you personally through His Word.

S T E P 5

Live in response.

Pinpoint what God is saying to you from this passage. How will you respond? Write what you will do now about what God has said to you. You might like to date it as a means not only of keeping a spiritual journal, but also of holding yourself accountable to following through in obedience.

Exercise: Mark 9:2-9

Work through Mark 9:2-9 on the next two pages using the approach just presented. Follow the instructions on the video presentation.

A completed example follows on pages 14-15. The exercise will be more beneficial to you if do not refer to the completed example until you work through the exercise on your own. After you work through the process, look at the example. Track each verse carefully through all five steps so you can see how the facts are developed into lessons which then unfold into personal questions.

God bless you as you seek to learn this simple yet effective method of communicating with Him.

Mark 9:2-9

S T E P 1  S T E P 2

Look in God's Word.

Begin by reading the passage of Scripture. Underline, circle, or otherwise mark text if it will aid your study.

Mark 9:2-9

2 After six days Jesus took Peter, James and John with him and led them up a high mountain, where they were all alone. There he was transfigured before them.

3 His clothes became dazzling white, whiter than anyone in the world could bleach them.

4 And there appeared before them Elijah and Moses, who were talking with Jesus.

5 Peter said to Jesus, "Rabbi, it is good for us to be here. Let us put up three shelters—one for you, one for Moses and one for Elijah."

6 (He did not know what to say, they were so frightened.)

7 Then a cloud appeared and enveloped them, and a voice came from the cloud: "This is my Son, whom I love. Listen to him!"

8 Suddenly, when they looked around, they no longer saw anyone with them except Jesus.

9 As they were coming down the mountain, Jesus gave them orders not to tell anyone what they had seen until the Son of Man had risen from the dead.

What does the Scripture say?

Make a verse-by-verse list of the most outstanding, obvious facts. Don't paraphrase; be literal as you list the facts.

2a Jesus took three disciples alone up a mountain. There He was transfigured.

3. His clothes became whiter than white

4. Elijah + Moses talked ē them.

5. Peter said to Jesus — let us put up 3 monuments. — for you, Moses, + Elijah

6. He was frightened

7. a cloud appeared + covered them + a voice "This is my Son. Listen to Him".

8. Suddenly, no one was there except Jesus with them.

9. Jesus told them not to say anything to anyone until He was risen from dead.

S T E P **3**

What does the Scripture mean?

Identify a lesson to learn from each fact. Focus on spiritual lessons.

2a Jesus wants to be alone with us.

3. God's glory was shining thro Jesus — showing purity - vision was super-natural

in eternity Jesus is still face 4. Elijah & Moses are living — Talking - recognizable. *confirmed life after death* We should seek

5. Instead of putting up earthly monuments, we

we rush ahead & don't ask guidance

6. Sometimes we are frightened by what we hear.

7. God's word always points to Jesus

8. All we need is Jesus.

Now we can tell that Christ is present 9. Jesus does give specific orders — sometimes we are to keep precious thoughts to us individually until the time is right — ponder in our heart . . . . We have to come down from mt. & put into practice what we have learned

S T E P **5**   **Live in response.**
    Pinpoint what God is saying to you from this passage. How will you respond? Write down today's date and what you will do now about what He has said.

S T E P **4**

What does the Scripture mean to me?

Rewrite the lessons from step 3 in the form of questions. Be personal as you formulate your questions.

2a When do I make time to be alone with Jesus?

3. What is my vision of Jesus?

4. Do I talk to Jesus first?

5. Should I take time before speaking?

6. Am I sometimes frightened?

7. Do I see Him in Scripture?

8. When I am caught up in the moment, do I realize that Jesus is all that matters

9. How do I put into practice, what I have learned in the Word?

11/26/01 I am to make time to be alone with Jesus, talking to him first in my concerns, pondering what He is saying & putting it into practice.

Completed Example of Mark 9:2-9

S T E P 1

Look in God's Word.
Begin by reading the passage of Scripture. Underline, circle, or otherwise mark text if it will aid your study.

Mark 9:2-9

2 After six days Jesus took Peter, James and John with him and led them up a high mountain, where they were all alone. There he was transfigured before them.

3 His clothes became dazzling white, whiter than anyone in the world could bleach them.

4 And there appeared before them Elijah and Moses, who were talking with Jesus.

5 Peter said to Jesus, "Rabbi, it is good for us to be here. Let us put up three shelters—one for you, one for Moses and one for Elijah."

6 (He did not know what to say, they were so frightened.)

7 Then a cloud appeared and enveloped them, and a voice came from the cloud: "This is my Son, whom I love. Listen to him!"

8 Suddenly, when they looked around, they no longer saw anyone with them except Jesus.

9 As they were coming down the mountain, Jesus gave them orders not to tell anyone what they had seen until the Son of Man had risen from the dead.

S T E P 2

What does the Scripture say?
Make a verse-by-verse list of the most outstanding, obvious facts. Don't paraphrase; be literal as you list the facts.

2a Jesus took three disciples alone up a mountain.

2b-3 He was transfigured before them with clothes dazzling white.

4 Moses and Elijah appeared with Jesus.

5 Peter said three shelters should be put up.

6 He didn't know what to say.

7 A voice spoke from the cloud saying to listen to Jesus.

8 Suddenly they saw no one except Jesus.

9 They came down from the mountain.

STEP 3

What does the Scripture mean?
Identify a lesson to learn from each fact. Focus on spiritual lessons.

2a   Jesus wants to be alone with us.

2b-3 There are times we have to be alone with Jesus in order to have a vision of His glory.

4   The vision of His glory will be the focus of believers in eternity.

5   Instead of worshipping Christ, some who call themselves Christians want to build earthly monuments to His Name.

6   Sometimes our emotions prompt us to speak when we should be silent.

7   We are commanded by God to listen to what Jesus says.

8   When everything else fades away, including our visions and dreams of glory, our focus should still be on Jesus.

9   We eventually have to come down from the mountain.

STEP 4

What does the Scripture mean to me?
Rewrite the lessons from step 3 in the form of questions. Be personal as you formulate your questions.

2a   When do I make time to be alone with Jesus?

2b-3 What fresh vision of Jesus am I lacking because I don't spend time alone with Him each day?

4   How drastically will I have to adjust my focus from what it is today to what it will be one day in eternity?

5   What earthly monument - a ministry, a church, a denomination, a reputation - am I seeking to build instead of genuine worship of Christ?

6   When have I spoken out when I should have been silent in worship?

7   Having glimpsed the vision of His glory, how obedient am I to God's command to listen to the voice of His beloved Son?

8   Where is my focus?

9   What can I take from this experience back into my everyday life?

STEP 5   **Live in response.**
    Pinpoint what God is saying to you from this passage. How will you respond? Write down today's date and what you will do now about what He has said.

Jan. 8, 1999: I will begin today to make time each day to get alone with Jesus, read my Bible, and listen to His voice.

Hope When You Are Depressed

REVELATION 1: 1-19

Christ in you, the hope of glory.
Colossians 1:27b

"For I know the plans I have for you," declares
the Lord, "plans to prosper you and not to harm you,
plans to give you hope and a future."
Jeremiah 29:11

Worth Remembering

Spiritual discipline is an essential part of a person's ability to grow in his or her personal relationship with God through knowledge and understanding of His Word. The following worksheets enable you not only to discover for yourself the eternal truths revealed by God in the Bible, but also to hear God speaking personally through His Word. The Scripture you study will prepare you to participate in a meaningful small-group experience where you will use the viewer sheets during the video presentation and engage in discussion with other participants.

Revelation 1:1-3

S T E P 1

Look in God's Word.
Begin by reading the passage of Scripture. Underline, circle, or otherwise mark text if it will aid your study.

Revelation 1:1-3
1 The revelation of Jesus Christ, which God gave him to show his servants what must soon take place. He made it known by sending his angel to his servant John,

2 who testifies to everything he saw—that is, the word of God and the testimony of Jesus Christ.

3 Blessed is the one who reads the words of this prophecy, and blessed are those who hear it and take to heart what is written in it, because the time is near.

S T E P 2

What does the Scripture say?
Make a verse-by-verse list of the most outstanding, obvious facts. Don't paraphrase; be literal as you list the facts.

1 God gave the revelation of Jesus Christ, making it known to John to show His servants what would take place.

2. John testifies to the word of God & the testimony of Jesus Christ

3. Blessed is the one who reads these wor. & hear & take to heart what is written here The time is near.

STEP 3

What does the Scripture mean?
Identify a lesson to learn from each fact.
Focus on spiritual lessons.

1 God reveals Jesus to His servants through His
Word.

2. ~~John~~ We are testifying to
God's Word & His Son.

3. We will be blessed
when we read & hear
& put into practice
what is written.

STEP 4

What does the Scripture mean to me?
Rewrite the lessons from step 3 in the form
of questions. Be personal as you formulate
your questions.

1 Where am I looking for a fresh vision of
Jesus?

2. Do I tell others
about the Bible &
Jesus?

3. Am I receiving the
full blessing? Am
I doing what God's
word says?

STEP 5   Live in response.

Pinpoint what God is saying to you
from this passage. How will you respond?
Write down today's date and what you will
do now about what He has said.

11/27/01 I will seek to know
Am I seeking to know
Jesus & His Word.
Jesus & His Word better by
spending time with Him. I desire
to be obedient.

Revelation 1:4-8

STEP 1

Look in God's Word.

Begin by reading the passage of Scripture. Underline, circle, or otherwise mark text if it will aid your study.

Revelation 1:4-8

4 John, To the seven churches in the province of Asia: Grace and peace to you from him who is, and who was, and who is to come, and from the seven spirits before his throne,

5 and from Jesus Christ, who is the faithful witness, the firstborn from the dead, and the ruler of the kings of the earth. To him who loves us and has freed us from our sins by his blood,

6 and has made us to be a kingdom and priests to serve his God and Father—to him be glory and power for ever and ever! Amen.

7 Look, he is coming with the clouds,
    and every eye will see him,
even those who pierced him;
    and all the peoples of the earth will
    mourn because of him.
So shall it be! Amen.

8 "I am the Alpha and the Omega," says the Lord God, "who is, and who was, and who is to come, the Almighty."

STEP 2

What does the Scripture say?

Make a verse-by-verse list of the most outstanding, obvious facts. Don't paraphrase; be literal as you list the facts.

4-5a John greets seven churches with grace and peace from the Eternal, the seven-fold Spirit, and Jesus Christ.

5) Jesus is the firstborn, the faithful witness & ruler of the kings of the earth, who loves us & has freed us from our sins by his blood.

6.) He has made us to be a kingdom & priests to serve God the Father — to him be glory & power forever.

7) Jesus will come in the clouds & every eye will see him. It shall be to all people, even those who pierced him

8.) The Lord God is the first & the last, who is & was & is to come, the Almighty.

S T E P 3

What does the Scripture mean?
Identify a lesson to learn from each fact. Focus on spiritual lessons.

4-5a Grace and peace come from the triune God.

5.) Jesus loves us & has freed us from our sins by his blood.

6.) Jesus has made us to serve Him — He is glory & power forever

7.) Every eye will see Jesus coming in the clouds.

8.) The Lord God is the Almighty — the beginning & the end of what is, what was, & will to come.

S T E P 4

What does the Scripture mean to me?
Rewrite the lessons from step 3 in the form of questions. Be personal as you formulate your questions.

4-5a From where, what, or whom am I seeking peace?

5.) Do I believe that Jesus' blood has paid the price for my sins?

6.) Jesus is the all glory & power — of the Heavenly Father Do I serve Him as such?

7.) Am I expectedly waiting for Him to return?

8.) Do I know the extent of his power?

S T E P 5 **Live in response.**
Pinpoint what God is saying to you from this passage. How will you respond? Write down today's date and what you will do now about what He has said.

11/29/01

When I comprehend the power & majesty of Jesus & I yearn for his return, I can find peace in the blood he spilt for me.

Revelation 1:9-12a

STEP 1

STEP 2

Look in God's Word.

Begin by reading the passage of Scripture. Underline, circle, or otherwise mark text if it will aid your study.

Revelation 1:9-12a

9 I, John, your brother and companion in the suffering and kingdom and patient endurance that are ours in Jesus, was on the island of Patmos because of the word of God and the testimony of Jesus.

10 On the Lord's Day I was in the Spirit, and I heard behind me a loud voice like a trumpet,

11 which said: "Write on a scroll what you see and send it to the seven churches: to Ephesus, Smyrna, Pergamum, Thyatira, Sardis, Philadelphia and Laodicea."

12a I turned around to see the voice that was speaking to me.

What does the Scripture say?

Make a verse-by-verse list of the most outstanding, obvious facts. Don't paraphrase; be literal as you list the facts.

9 John was suffering patiently on the Isle of Patmos because of God's Word and the testimony of Jesus.

10) On the Lord's Day, John was in the Spirit & heard a loud voice like a trumpet

11) the Spirit told John to write on a scroll what he saw & send it to the 7 churches.

12a) John turned to see who was speaking to him.

STEP **3**

What does the Scripture mean?
Identify a lesson to learn from each fact.
Focus on spiritual lessons.

9 It is possible to suffer for doing the right
thing, yet endure it with patience.

10.) We can hear God
      speak loudly & clearly.

11.) The Spirit of God gives
      us instruction.

12.) The Voice made him
      turn to see who
      was speaking.

STEP **4**

What does the Scripture mean to me?
Rewrite the lessons from step 3 in the form
of questions. Be personal as you formulate
your questions.

9 What is my attitude when suffering unjustly?

10.) Can I hear God speaking
      to me?

11.) Do I sense the Holy
      Spirits' instruction?

12.) Am I obedient to His
      direction?

STEP **5**   **Live in response.**
     Pinpoint what God is saying to you
from this passage. How will you respond?
Write down today's date and what you will
do now about what He has said.

11/29/01 My prayer is... may
If I suffer unjustly, ~~will~~ may
my attitude allow me to hear
the instruction by the H.S. &
~~will~~ May I follow through in obedience.

Revelation 1:12b-16

Look in God's Word.

Begin by reading the passage of Scripture. Underline, circle, or otherwise mark text if it will aid your study.

Prayer

Revelation 1:12b-16

12b And when I turned I saw seven golden lampstands,

13 and among the lampstands was someone "like a son of man," dressed in a robe reaching down to his feet and with a golden sash around his chest.

14 His head and hair were white like wool, as white as snow, and his eyes were like blazing fire.

15 His feet were like bronze glowing in a furnace, and his voice was like the sound of rushing waters.

16 In his right hand he held seven stars, and out of his mouth came a sharp double-edged sword. His face was like the sun shining in all its brilliance.

What does the Scripture say?

Make a verse-by-verse list of the most outstanding, obvious facts. Don't paraphrase; be literal as you list the facts.

12b When John turned, he saw seven golden lampstands.

13. And John saw someone "like a son of man" in a long robe with a golden sash around his chest.

14. His head & hair were white as snow & his eye were blazing fire

15. His feet were glowing bronze & his voice like rushing waters.

16. He held 7 stars, & out of his mouth came a sharp dbl.-edged sword. His face shone like the sun.

STEP 3

What does the Scripture mean?
Identify a lesson to learn from each fact. Focus on spiritual lessons.

12b Turning toward God brings His identity into proper perspective.

13. Jesus is recognizable

14. Jesus is pure + he sees everything

15. Jesus' steps are easily tracked + his voice can not be silenced

16. He holds everything in his power & speaks TRUTH. His brilliance is like the sun.

STEP 4

What does the Scripture mean to me?
Rewrite the lessons from step 3 in the form of questions. Be personal as you formulate your questions.

12b Which direction should I turn to recognize God's presence in my life?

13. Am I able to see him at work in my life?

14. Do I realize that nothing is overlooked by him, for he sees my inner motives?

15. Can I sense His presence? Am I seeking to hear him? Am I listening?

16. Do I give Him full reign of my life? Do I reflect the "light"?

STEP 5 **Live in response.**
Pinpoint what God is saying to you from this passage. How will you respond? Write down today's date and what you will do now about what He has said.

12/01/01

I yearn to be so atuned to His presence & guidance in my life that I will reflect His love to others.

Revelation 1:17-19

STEP 1

Look in God's Word.

Begin by reading the passage of Scripture. Underline, circle, or otherwise mark text if it will aid your study.

Revelation 1:17-19

17 When I saw him, I fell at his feet as though dead. Then he placed his right hand on me and said: "Do not be afraid. I am the First and the Last.

18 I am the Living One; I was dead, and behold I am alive for ever and ever! And I hold the keys of death and Hades.

19 "Write, therefore, what you have seen, what is now and what will take place later."

STEP 2

What does the Scripture say?

Make a verse-by-verse list of the most outstanding, obvious facts. Don't paraphrase; be literal as you list the facts.

17 When John saw Jesus, he fell at His feet, felt His hand, and heard His voice telling him not to be afraid.

18. Jesus is alive forever, being raised from the grave. He holds the keys of death & hell.

19. Jesus instructs John to write what he has seen now & later.

S T E P 3

What does the Scripture mean?
Identify a lesson to learn from each fact.
Focus on spiritual lessons.

17 A genuine vision of Jesus Christ results in
awe-inspired worship and surrender, while His
Word brings reassuring peace.

18. Jesus was crucified, dead, & was raised and sits at the right hand of God the Father, judging every person.

19. The Bible has been written to reveal Jesus past, present, & future.

S T E P 4

What does the Scripture mean to me?
Rewrite the lessons from step 3 in the form
of questions. Be personal as you formulate
your questions.

17 What impact is the vision of Christ having
on my life?

18. Do I tell others of His grace, so freely given?

19. Do I study so that I am able to communicate clearly the gospel message?

S T E P 5   **Live in response.**
     Pinpoint what God is saying to you
from this passage. How will you respond?
Write down today's date and what you will
do now about what He has said.

12-01-01

I desire to begin seriously studying God's Word & hiding it in my heart to be able to speak clearly about Him.

Revelation 1:1-19

Responding to God

Focus on what God is saying to you from this section's Scripture
passages. Rewrite your responses below from each step 5 on
the previous pages.

Revelation 1:1-3

I will seek to know Jesus + His Word
better by spending time with Him.
I desire to be obedient.

Revelation 1:4-8

When I comprehend the power + majesty
of Jesus + I yearn for His return, I can
find peace in the blood he spilt for me.

Revelation 1:9-12a

My prayer is, if I suffer unjustly, may
my attitude allow me to hear instruction from
the H.S. + may I follow thro in obedience.

Revelation 1:12b-16

I yearn to be so atuned to His presence +
guidance in my life that I will reflect
His love to others.

Revelation 1:17-19

I desire to seriously studying God's Word
+ hiding it in my heart to be able to speak
clearly about Him.

Prayerfully review your responses. What will you do now? Write
down today's date and what you will commit to do about what God
has said.

12/01/01

I committ to daily prayer & time alone with Jesus. I desire to be obedient, intent to hear his instruction & put into practice what I learn. I will seek to communicate clearly to others what I know.

Talk with God about your commitment. Pray for continued direction
and a deeper relationship with God.

VIDEO LISTENING SHEETS

Hope When You Are Depressed
Revelation 1:1-19

I. Refocus Through Prophecy—Revelation 1:1-3

Revelation of Jesus Christ

Gen 3:15 prophecy - seed

" 12 seed

Moses -

Isa

49 "I saw"

28 "I heard"

Book of Rev :

a "fresh vision" of J.C. to give up <u>HOPE</u> — Get your

focus off <u>yourself</u> — an onto Jesus

Gen. 1-1

vs 26

seven-fold Spirit : seven is

John's personal testimony Book of REV.

II. Refocus Through Praise—Revelation 1:4-8

Jesus is God Man

THE most important Man in the Universe forever.

You find your self-esteem in the person of J.C.

BEGIN PRAYER: Praise Him for His
          diety
       humanity
         Alpha & Omega – our wisdom
            omniscient
            omnipresent – who is, was, & is to come
            omnipetant

III. Refocus Through Preoccupation—Revelation 1:9-16

John - 90 yr. old
   assigned to manual labor
"Cut off" in exile – isolated – suffering
What is your Patmos?

John was preoccupied c̄ Christ
draw strength with being alone c̄ Christ

Revelation 1:1-19

VS 10 : God speaks thro His Word to us — make time to listen

VS 12 : John made committment — "turn around" — & rec. fresh Vision of God's glory.

    Jesus draws near to those who are willing to turn around.

vs 13 : there are no "accidents" with Jesus

vs 14 : "ancient of days" — wisdom

    15 — Jesus angry at what goes on in life that causes you stress.

vs 16 —

    "sharp dbl-edge sword - His Word
focus on Jesus

IV. Refocus Through Prostration—Revelation 1:17-19

vs 17   fall at feet of Jesus in silence (as a dead man)
absolutely still — no longer resisting H.S.

    "surrender afresh — be quiet & still before Him.

SEMINAR 2

Hope When You Are Deluded

REVELATION 2:1-7; 3:1-22

Everyone who has this hope in him purifies
himself, just as he is pure.
1 John 3:3

I pray also that the eyes of your heart may be
enlightened in order that you may know
the hope to which he has called you.
Ephesians 1:18a

Worth Remembering

Spiritual discipline is an essential part of a person's ability to
grow in his or her personal relationship with God through
knowledge and understanding of His Word. The following
worksheets enable you not only to discover for yourself the
eternal truths revealed by God in the Bible, but also to hear
God speaking personally through His Word. The Scripture you
study will prepare you to participate in a meaningful small-
group experience where you will use the viewer sheets during
the video presentation and engage in discussion with other
participants.

Revelation 2:1-7

STEP 1

Look in God's Word.
Begin by reading the passage of Scripture. Underline, circle, or otherwise mark text if it will aid your study.

Revelation 2:1-7

1 "To the angel of the church in Ephesus write: These are the words of him who holds the seven stars in his right hand and walks among the seven golden lampstands:

2 I know your deeds, your hard work and your perseverance. I know that you cannot tolerate wicked men, that you have tested those who claim to be apostles but are not, and have found them false.

3 You have persevered and have endured hardships for my name, and have not grown weary.

4 Yet I hold this against you: <u>You have forsaken your first love.</u>

5 Remember the height from which you have fallen! <u>Repent</u> and <u>do the things you did at first.</u> If you do not repent, I will come to you and remove your lampstand from its place.

6 But you have this in your favour: You hate the practices of the Nicolaitans, which I also hate.

7 <u>He who has an ear, let him hear</u> what the Spirit says to the churches. <u>To him who overcomes, I will give the right to eat from the tree of life,</u> which is in the paradise of God."

STEP 2

What does the Scripture say?
Make a verse-by-verse list of the most outstanding, obvious facts. Don't paraphrase; be literal as you list the facts.

1 The <u>One</u> who holds the stars and walks amongst the lampstands writes a word to the <u>Ephesian</u> church.

2.) I know your deeds, hard works & perseverance. You cannot tolerate wicked men & you test them & find them false.

3.) In your perseverance you have endured hardships for me & not grown weary.

4.) Yet, you have forsaken your first love.

5.) Remember, where you came from! Repent & turn back, for you risk removal of your lampstand.

6.) You hate the practices of the Nicolaitans, just as I do.

7.) He who has an ear, listen to what the Spirit says to the church. When you do this, ~~I will g~~ you will be able to eat from the tree of life in paradise.

STEP 3

What does the Scripture mean?
Identify a lesson to learn from each fact.
Focus on spiritual lessons.

1 Through His written Word, Jesus reveals His
presence in our midst.

2.) Jesus sees our deeds, works, & perserverance. He sees how we test wickedness against His ways.

3.) Jesus will give us strength to perservere.

4.) But NEVER forsake your love for Jesus — this should comes first in your life.

5) We risk seperation from God, if we do not repent, and return to Him.

6) Jesus hates worldliness.

7.) Listen to the Spirit for guidance so that we can overcome sin & dwell with Him forever.

STEP 4

What does the Scripture mean to me?
Rewrite the lessons from step 3 in the form
of questions. Be personal as you formulate
your questions.

1 If I lack an awareness of His presence in my
life, could it be because I have neglected my
Bible reading?

2.) Am I able to distinguish between good & evil based on God's principals?

3) Do I rely fully on God for strength & endurance?

4.) Is Christ first in my life?

5) Have I confessed to Him my pre-occupation with "living"? I do not want to be seperated from Him

6) Have I committed myself to return to Him?

7.) Am I open to the Spirits' leading?

STEP 5 — Live in response.

Pinpoint what God is saying to you
from this passage. How will you respond?
Write down today's date and what you will do
now about what He has said.

12/5/01
I will look to my heavenly Father for strength to endure changes in my life that need to be made — consistancy to study God's Word and make Christ first in everything. I desire the Holy Spirit to guide me.

Revelation 3:1-6

S T E P 1

Look in God's Word.
Begin by reading the passage of Scripture. Underline, circle, or otherwise mark text if it will aid your study.

Revelation 3:1-6

1 "To the angel of the church in Sardis write: These are the words of him who holds the seven spirits of God and the seven stars. I know your deeds; you have a reputation of being alive, but you are dead.
2 Wake up! Strengthen what remains and is about to die, for I have not found your deeds complete in the sight of my God.
3 Remember, therefore, what you have received and heard; obey it, and repent. But if you do not wake up, I will come like a thief, and you will not know at what time I will come to you.
4 Yet you have a few people in Sardis who have not soiled their clothes. They will walk with me, dressed in white, for they are worthy.
5 He who overcomes will, like them, be dressed in white. I will never blot out his name from the book of life, but will acknowledge his name before my Father and his angels.
6 He who has an ear, let him hear what the Spirit says to the churches."

S T E P 2

What does the Scripture say?
Make a verse-by-verse list of the most outstanding, obvious facts. Don't paraphrase; be literal as you list the facts.

1 The One who holds the Spirit of God and the stars knows the deeds and reputation of the church at Sardis.

2.) Wake up & strengthen what you do know, for I have not found your deeds worthy.

3.) Remember what you have received & heard; obey & repent for you do not know then I will come.

4.) A few will walk c̄ me, for they are worthy.

5.) If you overcome these ways, and live pure lives I will never blot you from the Book of life, but will acknowledge you before the Father.

6.) If you have ears, listen to the Spirit.

STEP 3

What does the Scripture mean?
Identify a lesson to learn from each fact.
Focus on spiritual lessons.

1 God is not impressed by our reputation.

2.) Awaken & strengthen yourselves, for God sees & knows all about you.

3.) Turn back to the truth, obey & repent. The hour is near.

4.) A few will walk c̄ God, worthy & spotless before him..... or not all will.....

5.) God desires <u>all</u> who live pure lives, to be acknowledged before Him & their names written in the book of life.

6.) Open my ears & listen to the Holy Spirit.

STEP 4

What does the Scripture mean to me?
Rewrite the lessons from step 3 in the form
of questions. Be personal as you formulate
your questions.

1 How closely does my reputation before others resemble what God knows to be accurate?

2.) ~~Does~~ what God sees in me, ~~who~~ an accurate picture of what the world sees me do?

3.) Be prepared! Am I obedient and repentant in my heart?

4.) Am I maturing in my walk c̄ God?

5. Do I live my life with hope & faith that I ~~am~~ am certain of my eternity?

6.) Am I open to hearing & listening to the Holy Spirit?

STEP 5   **Live in response.**
Pinpoint what God is saying to you
from this passage. How will you respond?
Write down today's date and what you will do
now about what He has said.

12/06/01

I am praying that I am atuned to the Spirits' promptings & that I take time to listen as I desire to Strengthen My walk c̄ God. I walk to be ready & prepared to enter Heaven at the blink of an eye.

Revelation 3:7-13

STEP 1

Look in God's Word.
Begin by reading the passage of Scripture. Underline, circle, or otherwise mark text if it will aid your study.

Revelation 3:7-13

7 "To the angel of the church in Philadelphia write: These are the <u>words of him</u> who is holy and true, <u>who holds the key of David</u>. What he opens no one can shut, and what he shuts no one can open.

8 <u>I know</u> your deeds. See, <u>I have placed</u> before you an open door that no one can shut. <u>I know</u> that you have little strength, <u>yet you have kept my word and have not denied my name.</u>

9 I will make those who are of the synagogue of Satan, who claim to be Jews though they are not, but are liars—I will <u>make them come and fall down at your feet and acknowledge that I have loved you.</u>

10 <u>Since you have kept my command to endure patiently, I will also keep you</u> from the hour of trial that is going to come upon the whole world to test those who live on the earth.

11 I am coming soon. Hold on to what you have, so that no one will take your crown.

12 Him who overcomes I will make a pillar in the temple of my God. Never again will he leave it. I will write on him the name of my God and the name of the city of my God, the new Jerusalem, which is coming down out of heaven from my God; and I will also write on him my new name.

13 He who has an ear, let him hear what the Spirit says to the churches.

STEP 2

What does the Scripture say?
Make a verse-by-verse list of the most outstanding, obvious facts. Don't paraphrase; be literal as you list the facts.

7 The One who holds the key of David opens and shuts the door.

8. God knows our deeds & has placed an open door before us. We have little strength of our own, yet keep His word & have not denied His name.

9. He will make the ungod fall down at your feet & acknowledge that I have loved you.

10. Because you have endured I will keep you from the hour of trial that will test those on the earth.

11. I am coming soon. Hold on to your crown

12. To you who overcomes He will reward & write on him the name of God & the new Jerusalem.

13. Listen to the Spirit's instruction

STEP 3

What does the Scripture mean?
Identify a lesson to learn from each fact.
Focus on spiritual lessons.

7 Jesus Christ is the One who determines
which doors of opportunity are opened and
shut for me.

8. If we keep His Word & do not deny His name, He provides us strength to take these opportunities.

9. Others will see God's hand of guidance upon us & know that He is with us.

10. God will protect us.

11. Jesus is coming soon... persevere.

12. He will reward us by identifying us as one of His own.

13. Pay attention & listen to the H.S.

STEP 4

What does the Scripture mean to me?
Rewrite the lessons from step 3 in the form
of questions. Be personal as you formulate
your questions.

7 To whom or to what am I looking to give me
an opportunity?

8. Do I recognize that Jesus provides my strength to see these opportunities?

9. Can others see how God is guiding my life?

10. Do I recognize God's hand of protection upon my life?

11. Do I await Christ's return with eager anticipation. Does it compel me toward maturity in Him?

12. Can I even image the reward awaiting me if I remain faithful?

13. Am I listening & waiting for His instruction?

STEP 5 — Live in response.
Pinpoint what God is saying to you
from this passage. How will you respond?
Write down today's date and what you will do
now about what He has said.

12/11/01

I pray that I see the H.S. working in my life to take advantage of every opportunity to share with others the joy of Christian life, to see His hand of protection & His drawing me closer to Himself.

39

Revelation 3:14-22

Look in God's Word.

Begin by reading the passage of Scripture. Underline, circle, or otherwise mark text if it will aid your study.

Revelation 3:14-22

14 "To the angel of the church in Laodicea write: These are the words of the Amen, the faithful and true witness, the ruler of God's creation.

15 I know your deeds, that you are neither cold nor hot. I wish you were either one or the other!

16 So, because you are lukewarm—neither hot nor cold—I am about to spit you out of my mouth.

17 You say, 'I am rich; I have acquired wealth and do not need a thing.' But you do not realize that you are wretched, pitiful, poor, blind and naked.

18 I counsel you to buy from me gold refined in the fire, so you can become rich; and white clothes to wear, so you can cover your shameful nakedness; and salve to put on your eyes, so you can see.

19 Those whom I love I rebuke and discipline. So be earnest, and repent.

20 Here I am! I stand at the door and knock. If anyone hears my voice and opens the door, I will come in and eat with him, and he with me.

21 To him who overcomes, I will give the right to sit with me on my throne, just as I overcame and sat down with my Father on his throne.

22 He who has an ear, let him hear what the Spirit says to the churches."

What does the Scripture say?

Make a verse-by-verse list of the most outstanding, obvious facts. Don't paraphrase; be literal as you list the facts.

14 The One who is the Amen, the witness, the ruler of creation, has a word for the church at Laodicea.

15.) Jesus knows your deed. & wishes you to be hot or cold.

16.) Because you are lukewarm, He is about to spit you out!

17.) If you think you are rich, you do not realize how wretched, poor, blind & naked you are.

18.) Jesus wants you to buy from him gold refined in the fire so you will be rich & white clothes to wear to cover your nakedness & healing salve to put on your blind eyes

19.) If I rebuke you, & discipline you, its because I love you – Be earnest & repent.

20.) Look! I stand & knock @ your hearts door – if you open it I will come in & fellowship ∴

21.) If you overcome, you will sit & rule on my Fathers throne

22.) Listen to the Spirit!

STEP 3

What does the Scripture mean?
Identify a lesson to learn from each fact. Focus on spiritual lessons.

14 Jesus is the Amen—He will have the last word.

15.) Jesus sees our deeds & knows our motives.

16.) If you are lukewarm, neither hot nor cold, He grows impatient.

17.) We do not recognize our own spiritual condition

18.) Jesus wants to help us live a spotless life & to see Him.

19.) If we are earnest & repent, He disciplines because He loves us.

20.) Jesus will come into our life & fellowship if we invite Him in.

21.) Your reward will be great if you follow me.

22.) Listen, open the door & follow me.

STEP 4

What does the Scripture mean to me?
Rewrite the lessons from step 3 in the form of questions. Be personal as you formulate your questions.

14 Do I acknowledge the final authority of God's Word?

15.) Do I realize nothing I do can be overlooked by Him?

16.) Is He about to spit me out for my lukewarmness?

17.) Do I think more highly of myself & am blinded by my lack of discipline?

18.) Am I letting Him help direct my steps?

19.) Can I see His discipline? Am I earnestly repentant?

20.) Does He hear my cry for fellowship c̄ Him?

21.) Do I look for the reward I will have c̄ Him by being obedient?

22.) Am I listening, ready to follow wherever He leads?

STEP 5 **Live in response.** 12-14-01
Pinpoint what God is saying to you from this passage. How will you respond? Write down today's date and what you will do now about what He has said.

Will I ever have a consistent, Spirit-led walk & grow mature in my relationship with Him?

Lord, help me to die to self & focus on you.

41

Revelation 2:1-7; 3:1-22

Responding to God

Focus on what God is saying to you from this section's Scripture
passages. Rewrite your responses below from each step 5 on
the previous pages.

Revelation 2:1-7 I will look to my heavenly Father for
strength to endure changes in my life that
need to be made — consistancy to Study God's
Word & make Christ first in my life. I desire
the Holy Spirit to guide me.

Revelation 3:1-6 I am praying that I am atuned to
the Spirit's promptings & that I take time to
listen as I desire to strengthen my walk c̄ God.
I want to be ready & prepared to enter Heaven
at the blink of an eye.

Revelation 3:7-13 I pray that I see the H.S. working in
my life to take advantage to share of every
opportunity to share with others the joy of Christian
life, to see the hand of protection & His drawing
me closer to Himself.

Revelation 3:14-22 Will I ever have a consistant, Spirit-
led walk & grow mature in my relationship
with Him? Lord help me to die to self & focus
on you.

Prayerfully review your responses. What will you do now? Write
down today's date and what you will commit to do about what God
has said.   12/15

I desire to die to self & focus on Him.

Talk with God about your commitment. Pray for continued direction
and a deeper relationship with God.

Revelation 2:1-7; 3:1-22

Hope When You Are Deluded
Revelation 2:1-7; 3:1-22

I. Deluded by Busyness—Revelation 2:1-7

Hope When You Are Deluded

Revelation 2:1-7; 3:1-22

III. Deluded by Weakness—Revelation 3:7-13

IV. Deluded by Religiousness—Revelation 3:14-22

Revelation 2:1-7; 3:1-22

SEMINAR 3

Hope When You Are Discouraged

REVELATION 4–5

> "Now, Lord, what do I look for?
> My hope is in you."
> *Psalm 39:7*
>
> As for me, I will always have hope.
> *Psalm 71:14*

Worth Remembering

Spiritual discipline is an essential part of a person's ability to grow in his or her personal relationship with God through knowledge and understanding of His Word. The following worksheets enable you not only to discover for yourself the eternal truths revealed by God in the Bible, but also to hear God speaking personally through His Word. The Scripture you study will prepare you to participate in a meaningful small-group experience where you will use the viewer sheets during the video presentation and engage in discussion with other participants.

Revelation 4:1-3a

Look in God's Word.
Begin by reading the passage of Scripture.
Underline, circle, or otherwise mark text if
it will aid your study.

Revelation 4:1-3a

1 After this I looked, and there before me
was a door standing open in heaven. And
the voice I had first heard speaking to me
like a trumpet said, "Come up here, and I
will show you what must take place after
this."

2 At once I was in the Spirit, and there
before me was a throne in heaven with
someone sitting on it.

3a And the one who sat there had the
appearance of jasper and carnelian.

What does the Scripture say?
Make a verse-by-verse list of the most outstanding, obvious facts. Don't paraphrase;
be literal as you list the facts.

1 John saw heaven opened and heard a voice
telling him to come and be shown what
would take place.

2. John was in the Spirit
emmediatly & saw
someone sitting on a
throne in heaven.

3a. The one sitting there
had the appearance
of jasper & carnelian
(precious stones)

God has the
appearance of
precious gems.

STEP 3

What does the Scripture mean?
Identify a lesson to learn from each fact. Focus on spiritual lessons.

1 Through His Word, God reveals His plans and purposes to those who serve Him.

2. The Word speaks to us personally.

3a. We can have a vision of heaven when we obey Him.

STEP 4

What does the Scripture mean to me?
Rewrite the lessons from step 3 in the form of questions. Be personal as you formulate your questions.

1 Do my present and future circumstances seem confusing or frightening because I have neglected my Bible reading, and do not know what God is doing?

2.) Do I apply & listen to Him through the reading of His Word?

3a) How can I "see" Him if I am not consistant in the study of His Word?

STEP 5   Live in response.
Pinpoint what God is saying to you from this passage. How will you respond? Write down today's date and what you will do now about what He has said.

1/02/02

I have not been consistant in reading & studying God's Word, therefore I can not see His leading me in a specefic direction. I desire to change & yield to discipline.

Revelation 4:3b-8a

STEP 1

Look in God's Word.
Begin by reading the passage of Scripture. Underline, circle, or otherwise mark text if it will aid your study.

Revelation 4:3b-8a

all believers

3b A rainbow, resembling an emerald, encircled the throne. / *12 tribes + 12 apostles*

4 Surrounding the throne were twenty-four other thrones, and seated on them were twenty-four elders. They were dressed in white and had crowns of gold on their heads.

5 From the throne came flashes of lightning, rumblings and peals of thunder. Before the throne, seven lamps were blazing. These are the seven spirits of God. *"seven" perfect number*

6 Also before the throne there was what looked like a sea of glass, clear as crystal. In the center, around the throne, were four living creatures, and they were covered with eyes, in front and in back.

7 The first living creature was like a lion, the second was like an ox, the third had a face like a man, the fourth was like a flying eagle.

8a Each of the four living creatures had six wings and was covered with eyes all around, even under his wings. *(attributes of God)*

Four living creatures represent 4 attributes of God.
lion - majesty
ox - faithfulness
man - intell.
eagle - Sovereignty

STEP 2

What does the Scripture say?
Make a verse-by-verse list of the most outstanding, obvious facts. Don't paraphrase; be literal as you list the facts.

3b An emerald rainbow circles the throne.

4. Twenty-four elders were seated on thrones, dressed in white c̄ crowns of gold.

5. Lightening + thunder came from the throne. + seven lamps burning. These are the seven spirits of God.

6. A Sea of glass was before the throne + 4 living creatures covered with eyes were around it.

7. The creatures were like a lion, an ox, a man's face, + a flying eagle.

8a. Each had 6 wings + were covered with eyes.

ST E P 3

What does the Scripture mean?
Identify a lesson to learn from each fact. Focus on spiritual lessons.

3b God's mercy and our security are evident when He is in absolute authority.

4. God places those worthy of authority over us.

5. Lightening & Thunder could not move the Spirit of God. (Natural forces . . . .)

6. God sees all we do.

7. The Spirit of God is everywhere & has no limitations.

8. The Spirit of God sees all.

ST E P 4

What does the Scripture mean to me?
Rewrite the lessons from step 3 in the form of questions. Be personal as you formulate your questions.

3b If I am doubting God's mercy, or fearful of losing my eternal security, then who is sitting on the throne of my life?

4. Do I heed the teachings of Godly men/women that I am priviledged to hear?

5. Do I realize there is no escaping from the Spirit of God?

6. ~~Do I want the Spirits~~ Do I fully realize there is ~~no escaping~~ the H.S. Knows my thoughts, as well as my deeds?

7.

8. He cares for me in all things

ST E P 5   Live in response.
Pinpoint what God is saying to you from this passage. How will you respond? Write down today's date and what you will do now about what He has said.

1/03/02

I am ~~more~~ realizing more the power of the H.S. to lead & guide me. I pray to be more attentive to Him.

Revelation 4:8b-11

STEP 1

STEP 2

Look in God's Word.

Begin by reading the passage of Scripture. Underline, circle, or otherwise mark text if it will aid your study.

Revelation 4:8b-11

8b Day and night they never stop saying:
"Holy, holy, holy
is the Lord God Almighty,
who was, and is, and is to come."
9 Whenever the living creatures give glory, honor and thanks to him who sits on the throne and who lives for ever and ever,
10 the twenty-four elders fall down before him who sits on the throne, and worship him who lives for ever and ever. They lay their crowns before the throne and say:
11 "You are worthy, our Lord and God,
to receive glory and honor and power,
for you created all things,
and by your will they were created
and have their being."

What does the Scripture say?

Make a verse-by-verse list of the most outstanding, obvious facts. Don't paraphrase; be literal as you list the facts.

8b They never stop saying, "Holy is the Lord."

9. They give glory, honor & thanks to the Lord. Who lives forever & seats on the throne.

10. The elders fall down & worship him, laying their crowns before hi

11. They say, You are worthy to receive glory, honor & power. You created all things by your will.

STEP 3

What does the Scripture mean?
Identify a lesson to learn from each fact.
Focus on spiritual lessons.

8b Our worship of the Lord should never
cease.

9. We should give glory,
honor & thanks to
Him, who sits on
the throne forever.

10. Every good thing
comes from Him.

11. We are to glorify
& give thanks to
Him in all things

STEP 4

What does the Scripture mean to me?
Rewrite the lessons from step 3 in the form
of questions. Be personal as you formulate
your questions.

8b What has interrupted my worship of Christ?

9. Do I give glory, honor,
& thanks to Him in
everything?

10. Do I always remember
that everything good comes
from Him?

11. Do I give glory &
thanks to Him in
all things?

STEP 5 **Live in response.**
Pinpoint what God is saying to you
from this passage. How will you respond?
Write down today's date and what you will
do now about what He has said.

1/04/02

In my day to day living,
I want to remember first,
that Jesus Christ is worthy
of glory, honor & thanksgiving
of all that I have received
yesterday, today & tomorrow.

Revelation 5:1-8

STEP 1

Look in God's Word.

Begin by reading the passage of Scripture. Underline, circle, or otherwise mark text if it will aid your study.

Revelation 5:1-8

title deed to the world

what is going to happen

1 Then I saw in the right hand of him who sat on the throne a scroll with writing on both sides and sealed with seven seals.

2 And I saw a mighty angel proclaiming in a loud voice, "Who is worthy to break the seals and open the scroll?"

3 But no one in heaven or on earth or under the earth could open the scroll or even look inside it.

4 I wept and wept because no one was found who was worthy to open the scroll or look inside.

5 Then one of the elders said to me, "Do not weep! See, the Lion of the tribe of Judah, the Root of David, has triumphed. He is able to open the scroll and its seven seals."

6 Then I saw a Lamb, looking as if it had been slain, standing in the center of the throne, encircled by the four living creatures and the elders. He had seven horns and seven eyes, which are the seven spirits of God sent out into all the earth.

7 He came and took the scroll from the right hand of him who sat on the throne.

8 And when he had taken it, the four living creatures and the twenty-four elders fell down before the Lamb. Each one had a harp and they were holding golden bowls full of incense, which are the prayers of the saints.

STEP 2

What does the Scripture say?

Make a verse-by-verse list of the most outstanding, obvious facts. Don't paraphrase; be literal as you list the facts.

1 The One who sits on the throne holds in his hand a scroll with writing and seals.

2. A mighty angel said, WHO is worthy to break the seals & open the scroll

3. No one could open or look at it.

4. John wept because no one was found to be worthy.

5. Then the elder said to John, the Lion of Judah the Root of David is able to open the scroll & Seals.

6. The slain Lamb stood in the center of the throne.

7. The Lamb took the scroll from the One on the throne.

8. The 4 creatures & the 24 Elders worshiped the Lamb.

STEP 3

What does the Scripture mean?
Identify a lesson to learn from each fact. Focus on spiritual lessons.

1 There is Someone sitting on the throne at the center of the universe.

2. The angel is seeking the Worthy One to open the scroll.

3. No one was worthy.

4. We cannot look to man's intelligence.

5. Only Jesus Christ can fill our needs

6. He stands & waits for us to come to Him.

7. God sent His own Son for us.

8. the Prayers of the Saints go before us to the Throne of grace.

STEP 4

What does the Scripture mean to me?
Rewrite the lessons from step 3 in the form of questions. Be personal as you formulate your questions.

1 What difference does the knowledge that there is an actual physical Person who rules the universe make in my daily life?

2. Do I look to Jesus first for wisdom?

3. Do I rely upon Him only?

4. Do I realize man's limitations?

5. Do I understand that Jesus is the only one who can fill all my needs?

6. Do I wait upon His timing?

7. Do I have a close personal relationship with Him?

8. Do I ask other believers to pray for me?

STEP 5 **Live in response.**
Pinpoint what God is saying to you from this passage. How will you respond? Write down today's date and what you will do now about what He has said.

1-7-02

my love & devotion. needs

I can take my concerns to the One worthy person of Jesus Christ, who is able to meet my needs ... realizing that He is worthy of

Revelation 5:9-14

S T E P 1

Look in God's Word.

Begin by reading the passage of Scripture. Underline, circle, or otherwise mark text if it will aid your study.

Revelation 5:9-14

9 And they sang a new song: "You are worthy to take the scroll and to open its seals, because you were slain, and with your blood you purchased men for God from every tribe and language and people and nation.

10 You have made them to be a kingdom and priests to serve our God, and they will reign on the earth."

11 Then I looked and heard the voice of many angels, numbering thousands upon thousands, and ten thousand times ten thousand. They encircled the throne and the living creatures and the elders.

12 In a loud voice they sang: "Worthy is the Lamb, who was slain, to receive power and wealth and wisdom and strength and honor and glory and praise!"

13 Then I heard every creature in heaven and on earth and under the earth and on the sea, and all that is in them, singing: "To him who sits on the throne and to the Lamb be praise and honor and glory and power, for ever and ever!"

14 The four living creatures said, "Amen," and the elders fell down and worshiped.

S T E P 2

What does the Scripture say?

Make a verse-by-verse list of the most outstanding, obvious facts. Don't paraphrase; be literal as you list the facts.

9 They sang a new song about the worthiness of Christ to take the scroll, because He was slain and purchased men with His blood.

10. Christ has made a Kingdom & priests to serve God & reign.

11. John saw the host of angels encircling the throne.

12. The angels sang, that the Lamb, slain is worthy to receive power & wealth & wisdom & strength & honor & glory & praise.

13. Every creature in heaven & earth praised the Lamb forever.

14. The 4 living creatures & the elders fell down & worshiped.

Worship : anything that directs my full attention to God —

STEP 3

What does the Scripture mean?
Identify a lesson to learn from each fact.
Focus on spiritual lessons.

9 For all eternity, the Cross of Christ will be reason for rejoicing.

10. Christ has provided for us on earth as well as in heaven

11. A host of angels are at His disposal.

12. The angels proclaim his worthiness.

13. Every creature will praise Him forever.

14. They will all fall down & worship Him.

STEP 4

What does the Scripture mean to me?
Rewrite the lessons from step 3 in the form of questions. Be personal as you formulate your questions.

9 In light of the Cross, what reason do I have for losing my joy?

10. Do I acknowledge that Christ can meet all my needs?

11. Can I image everything being orchestrated by Him?

12. Do I proclaim His worthiness to be worshipped?

13. Do I give Him credit for working in my life?

14. Do I worship Him fully?

STEP 5 Live in response.
Pinpoint what God is saying to you from this passage. How will you respond? Write down today's date and what you will do now about what He has said.

1/07/02

I will look to Jesus in every situation to try to comprehend His glory & give Him praise & worship.

Revelation 4–5

Responding to God

Focus on what God is saying to you from this section's Scripture
passages. Rewrite your responses below from each step 5 on
the previous pages.

Revelation 4:1-3a I have not been consistent in reading &
studying God's Word, therefore I can not see Him
leading me in a specific direction. I desire to
change & yield to discipline.

Revelation 4:3b-8a .... I am realizing more the power of the
Holy Spirit to lead & guide me. I pray to be
more attentive to Him.

Revelation 4:8b-11 In my day to day living, I want to
remember first, that Jesus Christ is worthy
of all glory, honor, & thanksgiving of all that
I have received yesterday, today, & tomorrow

Revelation 5:1-8 I can take my concerns to the One
worthy person of Jesus Christ, who is able to meet
my needs .... realizing that He is worthy of my
love & devotion.

Revelation 5:9-14 I will look to Jesus in every situation
to try to comprehend His glory and give Him
praise & worship.

Prayerfully review your responses. What will you do now? Write
down today's date and what you will commit to do about what God
has said.

1/08/02

I desire to worship and praise the Heavenly Father more sincerely & look to Him more in daily living. I desire to come under the discipline of His love that I may serve Him more.

Talk with God about your commitment. Pray for continued direction
and a deeper relationship with God.

Revelation 4–5

Hope When You Are Discouraged
Revelation 4–5

I. Jesus Is Supreme as Lord—Revelation 4

    A. Enthroned at the Center of the Universe
       Revelation 4:1-3a

    B. Encircled by a Court in Heaven
       Revelation 4:3b-8a

Revelation 4–5

C. Enveloped in a Crescendo of Praise
Revelation 4:8b-11

II. Jesus Is Sufficient as Lamb—Revelation 5

    A. Unequaled Position of Jesus Christ
       Revelation 5:1-5

    B. Undisputed Power of Jesus Christ
       Revelation 5:6-7

Revelation 4–5

C. Unsurpassed Praise of Jesus Christ
   Revelation 5:8-14

Hope When You Are Distressed

REVELATION 6–19

But the eyes of the Lord are on those who fear him,
  on those whose hope is in his unfailing love,
to deliver them from death and keep them alive in
  famine.

Psalm 33:18-19

Why are you downcast, O my soul?
  Why so disturbed within me?
Put your hope in God,
  for I will yet praise him,
  my Savior and my God.

Psalm 42:5

Worth Remembering

Spiritual discipline is an essential part of a person's ability to grow in his or her personal relationship with God through knowledge and understanding of His Word. The following worksheets enable you not only to discover for yourself the eternal truths revealed by God in the Bible, but also to hear God speaking personally through His Word. The Scripture you study will prepare you to participate in a meaningful small-group experience where you will use the viewer sheets during the video presentation and engage in discussion with other participants.

Revelation 11:15-19

Look in God's Word.
Begin by reading the passage of Scripture. Underline, circle, or otherwise mark text if it will aid your study.

Revelation 11:15-19

15 The seventh angel sounded his trumpet, and there were loud voices in heaven, which said: "The kingdom of the world has become the kingdom of our Lord and of his Christ, and he will reign for ever and ever."

16 And the twenty-four elders, who were seated on their thrones before God, fell on their faces and worshiped God,

17 saying: "We give thanks to you, Lord God Almighty, the One who is and who was, because you have taken your great power and have begun to reign.

18 The nations were angry; and your wrath has come. The time has come for judging the dead, and for rewarding your servants the prophets and your saints and those who reverence your name, both small and great—and for destroying those who destroy the earth."

19 Then God's temple in heaven was opened, and within his temple was seen the ark of his covenant. And there came flashes of lightning, rumblings, peals of thunder, an earthquake and a great hailstorm.

What does the Scripture say?
Make a verse-by-verse list of the most outstanding, obvious facts. Don't paraphrase; be literal as you list the facts.

15 A trumpet and loud voices in heaven said: "The world has become the kingdom of Christ and He will reign forever."

16. The elders seated before God fell & worshiped Him.

17. And they ~~said~~ gave thanks for God's power to reign.

18. God's wrath has come to judge the dead & reward the prophets & saints & all who reverence your name — even destroying those who destroy the earth.

19. His temple was opened & the ark of his covenant was seen. And all acts of nature responded

STEP 3

What does the Scripture mean?
Identify a lesson to learn from each fact. Focus on spiritual lessons.

15 One day the world that was made by the Lord at Creation and bought by Him at Calvary, will be reigned by Him.

16. Christians will fall down & worship Him.

17. And give thanks that He reigns

18. God's wrath will judge everyone. + reward faithful

19. All earth will respond to Him & His holiness.

God's glory fully displayed at that time.

STEP 4

What does the Scripture mean to me?
Rewrite the lessons from step 3 in the form of questions. Be personal as you formulate your questions.

15 How can I be hopeless when I consider what the world is really coming to?

16. Do I worship Him today?

17. Am I thankful knowing He will reign on earth someday?

18. Am I fearful of His eternal wrath? ← Do I keep confessing my sins up to date "short accounts"

19. Do I rejoice that one day all the earth, past & present will respond to Him?

STEP 5   Live in response.
Pinpoint what God is saying to you from this passage. How will you respond? Write down today's date and what you will do now about what He has said.

1/09/02
I rejoice ~~pray~~ that I can look forward to His reign on earth & escape eternal wrath. All the earth will rejoice & respond to His Holiness.

Revelation 15:1-5

S T E P 1

Look in God's Word.

Begin by reading the passage of Scripture. Underline, circle, or otherwise mark text if it will aid your study.

Revelation 15:1-5

1 I (saw) in heaven another great and marvellous sign: seven angels with the seven last plagues—last, because with them God's wrath is completed.

2 And I (saw) what looked like a (sea of glass mixed with fire) and, standing beside the sea, those who had been victorious over the beast and his image and over the number of his name. They held harps given them by God

judgement

martyrs

3 and (sang) the song of Moses the servant of God and the song of the Lamb:

"Great and marvellous are your deeds,
 Lord God Almighty.
Just and true are your ways,
 King of the ages.

EXIS: 12/19

4 (Who) will not fear you, O Lord,
 and bring glory to your name?
For you alone are holy.
All nations will come
 and worship before you,
for your righteous acts have been revealed."

5 After this I looked and in heaven the temple, that is, the tabernacle of the Testimony, was opened.

S T E P 2

What does the Scripture say?

Make a verse-by-verse list of the most outstanding, obvious facts. Don't paraphrase; be literal as you list the facts.

1 John saw seven angels with seven last plagues because God's wrath was complete.

2. He saw those who were victorious over the beast holding harps from God.

3. The victorius ones Sang "Great & Marvellous are your deeds, just & true are your ways, Lord & King of the ages.

4. Who will not fear & bring glory to your name, O Lord. You alone are holy. All Nations will worship you for your righteous acts are revealed.

5. John looked & saw the temple was opened.

STEP 3

What does the Scripture mean?
Identify a lesson to learn from each fact.
Focus on spiritual lessons.

1 God's wrath is thorough, complete, and final.

2. Those who claim Jesus will be rewarded by God.

3. Christians will sing of the greatness & justice of the King.

4. All the earth will fear & give glory to your revealed righteousness O Lord.

5. When we look to Christ, we will find Him.

STEP 4

What does the Scripture mean to me?
Rewrite the lessons from step 3 in the form
of questions. Be personal as you formulate
your questions.

1 Whom do I know who believes he or she can
sin and get by with it?

2. Is my reward on earth or waiting for me in heaven?

3. Do I praise Him fully?

4. Do I fully accept God's holiness?

5. Am I looking to Him in everything?

STEP 5 — Live in response.
Pinpoint what God is saying to you
from this passage. How will you respond?
Write down today's date and what you will
do now about what He has said.

1/10/02

Oh Lord, I desire to seek you fully & to praise you for your Holiness.

Revelation 19:1-8

Look in God's Word.
Begin by reading the passage of Scripture. Underline, circle, or otherwise mark text if it will aid your study.

Revelation 19:1-8

1 After this I heard what sounded like the roar of a great multitude in heaven shouting: "Hallelujah! Salvation and glory and power belong to our God,

2 for true and just are his judgments. He has condemned the great prostitute who corrupted the earth by her adulteries. He has avenged on her the blood of his servants."

3 Again they shouted: "Hallelujah! The smoke from her goes up for ever and ever."

4 The twenty-four elders and the four living creatures fell down and worshiped God, who was seated on the throne. And they cried: "Amen, Hallelujah!"

5 Then a voice came from the throne, saying: "Praise our God, all you his servants, you who fear him, both small and great!"

6 Then I heard what sounded like a great multitude, like the roar of rushing waters and like loud peals of thunder, shouting: "Hallelujah! For our Lord God Almighty reigns.

7 Let us rejoice and be glad and give him glory! For the wedding of the Lamb *Christ* has come, and his bride has made herself ready. *church*

8 Fine linen, bright and clean, was given *church* her to wear." (Fine linen stands for the righteous acts of the saints.)

What does the Scripture say?
Make a verse-by-verse list of the most outstanding, obvious facts. Don't paraphrase; be literal as you list the facts.

1-2a John heard a great multitude in heaven shouting: Hallelujah! Salvation, glory, and power belong to God Who is just in judgment.

2b. God has condemned those who corrupt the earth. He has avenged on her the blood of his servants.

3. The great multitude, shouted "Hallelujah! the ungodly will burn forever."

4. The elders & the 4 creatures fell down & worshiped God seated on the throne & cried "Amen Hallelujah"

5. From the throne a voice said "Praise our God, you servants who fear Him."

6. The multitudes shouted "Hallelujah — our God reigns"

7. Rejoice & be glad for His glory. The wedding of the Lamb & His bride are ready"

8. His bride was covered in the righteous acts of the saints

STEP 3

What does the Scripture mean?
Identify a lesson to learn from each fact.
Focus on spiritual lessons.

1-2a All heaven rejoices in the salvation of the
righteous and judgment of the wicked.

2b. God has condemned those
who are sinful. His judgement
is sure.

3. All heaven ~~should~~ agreed
the ungodly will not be
in heaven.

4. God sits on the throne &
deserves our praise.

5. All who fear Him will
praise Him.

6. He reigns forever. Multitudes acknowledge Him loudly

7. His glory reigns forever.

8. (look up "wedding of Lamb" Love, intimate joy & fidelity
& "his bride."
Jesus has provided a "robe of righteousness"
for us to wear so that we can come
into God's presence.

STEP 4

What does the Scripture mean to me?
Rewrite the lessons from step 3 in the form
of questions. Be personal as you formulate
your questions.

1-2a When have I caused heaven to rejoice
because I was instrumental in someone's
salvation?

2b Do I weep for the unsaved?

3. Am I motivated by the fact
there is a hell to step out
of my comfort zone & witness?

4. Do I praise Him because
He is on the throne?

5. Do I fearfully reverence
Him for Who He is?

6. Do I understand the
word "forever"?

7. Do I understand & grasp
that His glory reigns
forever?

8. Am I preparing for.
Do I realize how special these
robes of righteousness are that
God has prepared for me.

From this passage, God is
showing me that I need to be
intentional to witness to those
around me.

STEP 5   Live in response.   1/11/02
Pinpoint what God is saying to you
from this passage. How will you respond?
Write down today's date and what you will
do now about what He has said.

Revelation 19:9-16

STEP 1

Look in God's Word.

Begin by reading the passage of Scripture. Underline, circle, or otherwise mark text if it will aid your study.

Revelation 19:9-16

9 Then the <u>angel said</u> to me, "Write: 'Blessed are those who are invited to the wedding supper of the Lamb!'" And he added, "These are <u>the true words of God</u>."

10 At this I fell at his feet to worship him. But he said to me, "Do not do it! I am a fellow servant with you and with your brothers who hold to the testimony of Jesus. <u>Worship God!</u> For the <u>testimony of Jesus is the spirit of prophecy.</u>"

11 I saw <u>heaven standing open</u> and there before me was a <u>white horse</u>, whose rider is called <u>Faithful and True</u>. With justice he <u>judges and makes war.</u>

symbol of ruling over many nations

12 His eyes are like blazing (fire,) and on his head are many (crowns.) <u>He has a name written on him that no one knows but he himself.</u>

13 He is dressed in a robe dipped in blood, and <u>his name is the Word of God.</u>

hosts of angels

14 The "armies of heaven" were following him, (riding on) (white horses) and (dressed in) fine linen, white and clean.

Lord surely victor

15 Out of his mouth comes a sharp sword with which to strike down the nations. "He <u>will rule them with an iron scepter.</u>" He *GOD JUDGEMENTS* <u>treads the winepress of the fury of the wrath of God</u> Almighty.

Marti c look up

16 On his robe and on his thigh he has this name written: <u>KING OF KINGS AND LORD OF LORDS.</u>

STEP 2

What does the Scripture say?

Make a verse-by-verse list of the most outstanding, obvious facts. Don't paraphrase; be literal as you list the facts.

9 The angel gave John true words from God, instructing him to write a blessing to those invited to the wedding supper.

10. The angel would not let John worship himself but said to him "Worship God".

11. Heaven stood open & the white horses' rider, Faithful & True, judges & makes war.

12. The rider's eyes are like fire & he wears many crowns. No one knows the name written on him.

13. His name is the Word of God & he wears a robe dipped in blood.

14. Following him are the armies of heaven, dressed in clean white linen.

15. He will rule them with an iron scepter & treads the winepress of the fury of the wrath of God.

16. His name is written: King of Kings & Lord of Lords.

STEP 3

What does the Scripture mean?
Identify a lesson to learn from each fact.
Focus on spiritual lessons.

9 John needed assurance that those invited
to the wedding supper were to receive a
blessing from God.

10. Do not worship anyone other than God.

11. Heaven is for the faithful & true. Christ & judge.

12.

It is not the blood of Christ, but of those He has slain

13. All who come to Heaven have been purchased with blood.

14. Jesus blood cleanes us white as snow.

15. Jesus will rule.

16. Jesus is King of Kings & Lord of Lords.

STEP 5

Live in response.   1/14/01
Pinpoint what God is saying to you
from this passage. How will you respond?
Write down today's date and what you will
do now about what He has said.

STEP 4

What does the Scripture mean to me?
Rewrite the lessons from step 3 in the form
of questions. Be personal as you formulate
your questions.

9 At that moment, will I need to be assured
that the blessing offered is from God?

10. Am I worshipping any one or anything other than God?

11. Will I be ready to stand alone in Heaven?

12.

13. What makes me worthy of the spilt blood of Christ?

14. Will I be spotless one day & free from sin?

15. Do I desire to be with Jesus when he rules in Heaven?

16. Do I proclaim Him to be King of Kings & Lord of Lord in my life?

I desire to proclaim Him as King of Kings & Lord of Lords, the only One worthy of my praise

75

Revelation 6–19

Responding to God

Focus on what God is saying to you from this section's Scripture passages. Rewrite your responses below from each step 5 on the previous pages.

Revelation 11:15-19

Revelation 15:1-5

Revelation 19:1-8

Revelation 19:9-16

Prayerfully review your responses. What will you do now? Write down today's date and what you will commit to do about what God has said.

Talk with God about your commitment. Pray for continued direction and a deeper relationship with God.

VIDEO LISTENING SHEETS

Hope When You Are Distressed
Revelation 6–19

I. Jesus Christ Is in Charge—Revelation 6–18

    A. With Principles of Judgment—Revelation 6:1–9:21; 11:15-19

B. With Provision of Mercy—Revelation 7:1-17; 11:1-13; 12:10-12; 14:1-13

Revelation 6-19

C. With Power—Revelation 13:1-18; 14:6-20; 16:1-21

II. Jesus Christ Is Coming—Revelation 19

A. The Saints Rejoice Over the Destruction of the Wicked—Revelation 19:1-5

B. The Saints Rejoice at the Celebration of the Wedding—Revelation 19:6-10

Revelation 6–19

C. The Saints Rejoice as the Son Returns—Revelation 19:11-21

Hope When You Are Defeated

REVELATION 21

Hope does not disappoint us,
because God has poured out his love
into our hearts by the Holy Spirit,
whom he has given us.
Romans 5:5

If only for this life we have hope in Christ,
we are to be pitied more than all men.
1 Corinthians 15:19

Worth Remembering

Spiritual discipline is an essential part of a person's ability to grow in his or her personal relationship with God through knowledge and understanding of His Word. The following worksheets enable you not only to discover for yourself the eternal truths revealed by God in the Bible, but also to hear God speaking personally through His Word. The Scripture you study will prepare you to participate in a meaningful small-group experience where you will use the viewer sheets during the video presentation and engage in discussion with other participants.

Revelation 21:1-8

STEP 1

Look in God's Word.

Begin by reading the passage of Scripture. Underline, circle, or otherwise mark text if it will aid your study.

Revelation 21:1-8

1 Then I saw a new heaven and a new earth, for the first heaven and the first earth had passed away, and there was no longer any sea.

2 I saw the Holy City, the new Jerusalem, coming down out of heaven from God, prepared as a bride beautifully dressed for her husband.

3 And I heard a loud voice from the throne saying, "Now the dwelling of God is with men, and he will live with them. They will be his people, and God himself will be with them and be their God.

4 He will wipe every tear from their eyes. There will be no more death or mourning or crying or pain, for the old order of things has passed away."

5 He who was seated on the throne said, "I am making everything new!" Then he said, "Write this down, for these words are trustworthy and true."

6 He said to me: "It is done. I am the Alpha and the Omega, the Beginning and the End. To him who is thirsty I will give to drink without cost from the spring of the water of life.

7 He who overcomes will inherit all this, and I will be his God and he will be my son.

8 The cowardly, the unbelieving, the vile, the murderers, the sexually immoral, those who practice magic arts, the idolaters and all liars—their place will be in the fiery lake of burning sulphur. This is the second death."

STEP 2

What does the Scripture say?

Make a verse-by-verse list of the most outstanding, obvious facts. Don't paraphrase; be literal as you list the facts.

1 John saw a new heaven and earth, for the old had passed away.

2. John saw the new Jerusalem prepared as a bride beautifully dressed.

3. He heard a voice say that God c̄ live c̄ them & be their God.

4. God will make the old pass away & there will be no more death

5. He was seated on the throne & will make all things new. He told John to write this.

6. God said "It is done" He is the beginning & the end. He will give without cost to the thirsty.

7. You will inherit this & I will be your God.

8. The second death in the fiery lake is for all unbelievers.

STEP 3

What does the Scripture mean?
Identify a lesson to learn from each fact.
Focus on spiritual lessons.

1 One day everything we see around us will no longer exist.

2. We will see the new Jerusalem in all its beauty.

3. God will live with us & in us.

4. God will comfort us & there will be no more death.

5. The Word of God, written for us, is true.

6. Jesus will give to all who are thirsty, without cost, the water of life.

7. To those who believe, Christ will be their God.

8. There will be a second death for the unbelievers.

STEP 4

What does the Scripture mean to me?
Rewrite the lessons from step 3 in the form of questions. Be personal as you formulate your questions.

1 How much time am I spending on that which is going to perish?

2. How much do I look forward to Heaven?

3. Do I live as though others can see Christ in me?

4. What do I fear in this life?

5. How much time am I spending in the Word?

6. Jesus - the Holy Spirit - will help me understand what is written.

7. Do I act like a child of God?

8. How do I react to the thought of Hell for my family?

STEP 5   **Live in response.**
Pinpoint what God is saying to you from this passage. How will you respond? Write down today's date and what you will do now about what He has said.

1-16-02

I want to concentrate more fully on eternity values and how I can impact those around me to point the way.

Revelation 21:9-14

STEP 1

Look in God's Word.
Begin by reading the passage of Scripture. Underline, circle, or otherwise mark text if it will aid your study.

Revelation 21:9-14

9 One of the seven angels who had the seven bowls full of the seven last plagues came and said to me, "Come, I will show you the bride, the wife of the [Church] Lamb."

10 And he carried me away in the Spirit to a mountain great and high, and showed me the Holy City, Jerusalem, coming down out of heaven from God.

11 It shone with the glory of God, and its brilliance was like that of a very precious jewel, like a jasper, clear as crystal.

12 It had a great, high wall with twelve gates, and with twelve angels at the gates. On the gates were written the names of the twelve tribes of Israel.

13 There were three gates on the east, three on the north, three on the south and three on the west.

14 The wall of the city had twelve foundations, and on them were the names of the twelve apostles of the Lamb.

STEP 2

What does the Scripture say?
Make a verse-by-verse list of the most outstanding, obvious facts. Don't paraphrase; be literal as you list the facts.

Church

9 One of the angels showed John the Bride of the Lamb.

10. The angel carried John to a high mountain & showed him the Holy City.

11. Heaven displayed the glory of God & its brilliance.

12. The 12 tribes of Israel were written on its gates, guarded by 12 angels.

13. There were 3 gates facing each direction.

14. The wall of the city had 12 foundations, representing the 12 apostles.

S T E P 3

What does the Scripture mean?
Identify a lesson to learn from each fact.
Focus on spiritual lessons.

9 The Lamb is deeply, permanently, emotion-
ally involved in a love relationship.

10. Jesus wants us to have a vision of heaven.

11. He wants us to see His Glory.

12. Our names can be written in heaven.

13. Heaven spans all directions.

14. We are to look to the recorded writings of the apostles & learn from them.

S T E P 4

What does the Scripture mean to me?
Rewrite the lessons from step 3 in the form
of questions. Be personal as you formulate
your questions.

9 Am I a responsive and passionate bride with
eyes only for her Husband?

10. Do I keep this vision of heaven fresh in my mind & heart?

11. Is my prayer to catch the vision of His glory?

12. Can I envision the expanse of heaven?

13. Will the Book of Life contain the names of all my family?

14. How much time & effort do I place on studying His Word?

S T E P 5 **Live in response.**
Pinpoint what God is saying to you
from this passage. How will you respond?
Write down today's date and what you will
do now about what He has said.

1-17-02

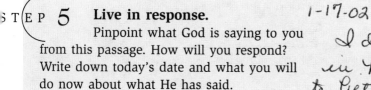

I desire to be more involved in knowing & studying His Word to better communicate the hope we have in heaven.

Revelation 21:15-21

STEP 1

Look in God's Word.
Begin by reading the passage of Scripture. Underline, circle, or otherwise mark text if it will aid your study.

New Jerusalem

Revelation 21:15-21

15 The <u>angel</u> who talked with me <u>had a measuring rod</u> of gold to measure the city, its gates and its walls.

16 <u>The city</u> was laid out like a <u>square</u>, as long as it was wide. He measured the city with the rod and found it to be <u>12,000 stadia in length,</u> and as wide and high as it is long.

1400 miles square

17 He measured its <u>wall</u> and it <u>was 144 cubits thick,</u> by man's measurement, which the angel was using.

200 ft. thick

18 The <u>wall was made of jasper,</u> and the <u>city of pure gold, as pure as glass.</u>

19 The <u>foundations</u> of the city walls were decorated with every kind of <u>precious stone.</u> The (first) foundation was jasper, the (second) sapphire, the (third) chalcedony, the (fourth) emerald,

20 the (fifth) sardonyx, the (sixth) carnelian, the seventh chrysolite, the (eighth) beryl, the (ninth) topaz, the (tenth) chrysoprase, the eleventh jacinth, and the (twelfth) amethyst.

21 The <u>twelve gates were twelve pearls,</u> each gate made of a <u>single</u> pearl. The great <u>street</u> of the city <u>was of pure gold,</u> like transparent glass.

STEP 2

What does the Scripture say?
Make a verse-by-verse list of the most outstanding, obvious facts. Don't paraphrase; be literal as you list the facts.

15 One of the angels had a measuring rod to measure the city.

16. The city was a square, 12,000 stadia in all directions.

17. Its walls were 144 cubits thick.

18. The wall was jasper & the city of pure gold.

19. The foundations were precious stones.

20. Each of the 12 foundation stones were different.

21. The 12 gates were each a pearl & the street was gold.

STEP 3

What does the Scripture mean?
Identify a lesson to learn from each fact.
Focus on spiritual lessons.

15 God provides a measuring rod through His
Word for my life.

16. He gives direction + dimention to my life.

17. He defends us.

18. He protects us.

19. He gives my life meaning.

20. He provides many pleasures for me to enjoy.

21. He defines my way.

STEP 4

What does the Scripture mean to me?
Rewrite the lessons from step 3 in the form
of questions. Be personal as you formulate
your questions.

15 Do I treat God's Word as a measuring rod
for my life?

16. Do I look for His directions in the Word?

17. Do I see how he looks after me?

18. Do I see His hand of protection around me?

19. Am I looking for His purpose for my life?

20. Am I thankful for the "jewels" he allows me?

21. Do I let Him lead me?

STEP 5   Live in response.

Pinpoint what God is saying to you
from this passage. How will you respond?
Write down today's date and what you will
do now about what He has said.

With confidence, I can
rely upon Christ to have
control of my life. His
word is true + he will not
leave me nor forsake me.

89

Revelation 21:22-27

STEP 1

Look in God's Word.
Begin by reading the passage of Scripture. Underline, circle, or otherwise mark text if it will aid your study.

Revelation 21:22-27
22 I did not see a temple in the city, because the Lord God Almighty and the Lamb are its temple.
23 The city does not need the sun or the moon to shine on it, for the glory of God gives it light, and the Lamb is its lamp.
24 The nations will walk by its light, and the kings of the earth will bring their splendor into it.
25 On no day will its gates ever be shut, for there will be no night there.
26 The glory and honor of the nations will be brought into it.
27 Nothing impure will ever enter it, nor will anyone who does what is shameful or deceitful, but only those whose names are written in the Lamb's book of life.

STEP 2

What does the Scripture say?
Make a verse-by-verse list of the most outstanding, obvious facts. Don't paraphrase; be literal as you list the facts.

22 The temple was not seen, because the Lord and the Lamb are the temple in the city.

23. There was no sun or moon for the glory of God gives light & the Lamb is its lamp.

24. Nations & Kings will be guided by God.

25. Heavens' gates will always be open & there will be no night.

26. Those from all nation will be there.

27. No one will be there except those who are written in the Lamb's book of life.

90

STEP 3

What does the Scripture mean?
Identify a lesson to learn from each fact.
Focus on spiritual lessons.

22 I will never lack an awareness of the presence of Christ in my life when I am in heaven.

23. There will be no need for the sun or moon, for Christ will be there.

24. Christ will be the example for all to follow.

25. Heaven is open to all.

26. All nationalities are free to come.

27. The Book of Life will contain the names of all who will be in heaven.

STEP 4

What does the Scripture mean to me?
Rewrite the lessons from step 3 in the form of questions. Be personal as you formulate your questions.

22 When lonely or discouraged, do I take comfort in the hope that one day I will be in His presence forever?

23. Is Christ the light of my life?

24. Do I look to Him only?

25. Do I tell others of Heaven?

26. Do I pray for other nations?

27. Do I witness to those around me?

STEP 5 Live in response.
Pinpoint what God is saying to you from this passage. How will you respond? Write down today's date and what you will do now about what He has said.

Revelation 21

Responding to God

Focus on what God is saying to you from this section's Scripture passages. Rewrite your responses below from each step 5 on the previous pages.

Revelation 21:1-8

Revelation 21:9-14

Revelation 21:15-21

Revelation 21:22-27

Prayerfully review your responses. What will you do now? Write down today's date and what you will commit to do about what God has said.

Talk with God about your commitment. Pray for continued direction and a deeper relationship with God.

Revelation 21

Hope When You Are Defeated
Revelation 21

I. Heaven Is a Prepared Place—Revelation 21:1-2

prepared as a Bride for her Husband

II. Heaven Is a Perfect Place—Revelation 21:3-8

no seperation
no scars.
no Suffering
no tears

III. Heaven Is a Physical Place—Revelation 21:9-21

15,000 miles square

200 ft. wide walls of jasper

a Safe place

a Stable place c̄ 12 foundations

Struggle of sin done away with

pearl gates – Christ's Suffering

Revelation 21

IV. Heaven Is a Populated Place—Revelation 21:22-27

Home of Lamb

We will live in the presence of Jesus forever

We will never be seperated from Him.

We will have overcome doubts
pride   } inherit Heaven
unbelief

Nothing impure

Lambs Book of Life : everyone born has name written there, but if you did not accept Christ, their names will be blotted out.

Heaven	Hell
No death mourning	Intense pain & suffering forever
Secure	Insecure
Stable	Unstable
Light	Darkness
Fellowship	Loneliness
Satisfaction	Dissatisfaction
With God forever	Eternal Seperation

Hope That Ignites Your Heart

REVELATION 22: 6-21

[The grace of God] teaches us to say "No"
to all ungodliness and worldly passions, and
to live self-controlled, upright and godly lives
in this present age, while we wait for
the blessed hope—the glorious appearing of our
great God and Savior, Jesus Christ.
Titus 2:12-13

Worth Remembering

Spiritual discipline is an essential part of a person's ability to grow in his or her personal relationship with God through knowledge and understanding of His Word. The following worksheets enable you not only to discover for yourself the eternal truths revealed by God in the Bible, but also to hear God speaking personally through His Word. The Scripture you study will prepare you to participate in a meaningful small-group experience where you will use the viewer sheets during the video presentation and engage in discussion with other participants.

Revelation 22:6-9

STEP 1

STEP 2

Look in God's Word.
Begin by reading the passage of Scripture. Underline, circle, or otherwise mark text if it will aid your study.

Revelation 22:6-9

6 The angel said to me, "These words are trustworthy and true. The Lord, the God of the spirits of the prophets, sent his angel to show his servants the things that must soon take place."

7 " 'Behold, I am coming soon! Blessed is he who keeps the words of the prophecy in this book.' "

8 I, John, am the one who heard and saw these things. And when I had heard and seen them, I fell down to worship at the feet of the angel who had been showing them to me.

9 But he said to me, "Do not do it! I am a fellow servant with you and with your brothers the prophets and of all who keep the words of this book. Worship God!"

What does the Scripture say?
Make a verse-by-verse list of the most outstanding, obvious facts. Don't paraphrase; be literal as you list the facts.

6 These words are true. The Lord sent His angel to show His servants what must take place.

7. I am coming soon! Keep the words of this book.

8. John heard & saw & worshiped at the feet of the angel.

9. The angel said not to worship him, but to worship God.

STEP 3

What does the Scripture mean?
Identify a lesson to learn from each fact.
Focus on spiritual lessons.

6 God does not lie, and He wants His servants
to have hope for the future.

7. The Lord Jesus promises to come soon & to bless those who keep His words

8. When we hear & see new insights, we are to worship & praise Him.

9. God is the only One worthy of our worship.

STEP 4

What does the Scripture mean to me?
Rewrite the lessons from step 3 in the form
of questions. Be personal as you formulate
your questions.

6 Is my hopelessness concerning the future
based on my doubt of the truth of God's
Word?

7. Am I awaiting the coming of Jesus by keeping in His Word?

8. Am I offering praise & worship as I gain new insights?

Sharon "No saint or angel - worship can have approval in Heaven"
9. Am I worshiping God fully?

Dee "What possessions, people, or things are keeping me from worshiping only the Lord?"

STEP 5 **Live in response.**
Pinpoint what God is saying to you
from this passage. How will you respond?
Write down today's date and what you will
do now about what He has said.

1-27-02

I desire to study & know His Word. & to praise Him & worship.

Revelation 22:10-15

STEP 1

STEP 2

Look in God's Word.
Begin by reading the passage of Scripture. Underline, circle, or otherwise mark text if it will aid your study.

Revelation 22:10-15

10 Then he told me, "Do not seal up the words of the prophecy of this book, because the time is near.
11 Let him who does wrong continue to do wrong; let him who is vile continue to be vile; let him who does right continue to do right; and let him who is holy continue to be holy."
12 " 'Behold, I am coming soon! My reward is with me, and I will give to everyone according to what he has done.
13 I am the Alpha and the Omega, the First and the Last, the Beginning and the End.
14 Blessed are those who wash their robes, that they may have the right to the tree of life and may go through the gates into the city.
15 Outside are the dogs, those who practice magic arts, the sexually immoral, the murderers, the idolaters and everyone who loves and practices falsehood.' "

What does the Scripture say?
Make a verse-by-verse list of the most outstanding, obvious facts. Don't paraphrase; be literal as you list the facts.

10 Don't seal this book, because the time is near.

11. Don't try to stop those doing wrong, but let those continue to do right & be holy.

12. I am coming Soon. My reward is with me.

13. I am the Beginning & the End.

14. Blessed are those who are clean from sin.

15. Outside the gates are the unholy ones.

STEP 3

What does the Scripture mean?
Identify a lesson to learn from each fact.
Focus on spiritual lessons.

10 As the end of human history draws near,
we will do well to read, study, and apply the
Book of Revelation.

11. Encourage those who follow Jesus.

12. Jesus will reward those who claim Him for their own.

13. Jesus is the First & the Last - He is Complete.

14. Blessed are the saved.

15. The unsaved are outside His protection.

STEP 4

What does the Scripture mean to me?
Rewrite the lessons from step 3 in the form
of questions. Be personal as you formulate
your questions.

II Tim 4:7

10 How much time have I given to reading,
studying and applying the Book of Revelation? See "will I become faint-hearted
So that I will finish well?"

11. Am I encouraging anyone to follow Jesus.

12. Am I storing up treasures in heaven?

13. Is He all that I'm trusting in?

14. Is He pouring out His blessings on my life now?

15. Do I weep for those still lost?

STEP 5 **Live in response.**   1/27/02

Pinpoint what God is saying to you
from this passage. How will you respond?
Write down today's date and what you will
do now about what He has said.

I desire to encourage others by studying more myself, but have failed miserably this week!

Revelation 22:16-21

STEP 1

Look in God's Word.
Begin by reading the passage of Scripture. Underline, circle, or otherwise mark text if it will aid your study.

Revelation 22:16-21
16 " 'I, Jesus, <u>have sent</u> my angel to give you this testimony for the churches. I am the Root and the Offspring of David, and the bright Morning Star.' "

17 <u>The Spirit</u> and <u>the bride</u> *church* say, "Come!" And let him who hears say, "Come!" <u>Whoever is thirsty</u>, let him come; and <u>whoever wishes</u>, let him take the <u>free gift of the water of life.</u>

18 I warn everyone who hears the words of the prophecy of this book: <u>If anyone adds anything to them, God will add to him the plagues</u> described in this book.

19 And if <u>anyone takes words away from this book</u> of prophecy, <u>God will take away from him his share in the tree of life and in the holy city</u>, which are described in this book.

20 He who testifies to these things says, " 'Yes, <u>I am coming soon</u>.' " Amen. <u>Come, Lord Jesus.</u>

21 The grace of the Lord Jesus be with God's people. Amen.

STEP 2

What does the Scripture say?
Make a verse-by-verse list of the most outstanding, obvious facts. Don't paraphrase; be literal as you list the facts.

16 Jesus, the Offspring of David, the Morning Star, sent His angel to give this testimony to the church.

17. The Spirit & the church say "Come" whoever is thirsty, & whoever wishes to have the free gift of the water of life.

18. If anyone adds to the words of this book, God will add to him the plagues

19. If anyone takes words away, God will take away his share in the tree of life & in the holy city.

20. "I am coming soon" Amen

21. Grace be with God's people — Amen.

Ask God to speak to our hearts before reading His Word, time.

STEP 3

What does the Scripture mean?
Identify a lesson to learn from each fact.
Focus on spiritual lessons.

16 The Book of Revelation was given specifically by Christ to those who call themselves by His name.

17. The Spirit calls to us to receive the free gift of Salvation.

18. Do not dare add any words to this Book.

19. Do not dare take away any words from this Book.

20. The Lord Jesus is coming Soon.

21. Grace will be given God's people.

STEP 5   Live in response.   1-28-02
Pinpoint what God is saying to you from this passage. How will you respond? Write down today's date and what you will do now about what He has said.

STEP 4

What does the Scripture mean to me?
Rewrite the lessons from step 3 in the form of questions. Be personal as you formulate your questions.

16 If I am one of those to whom the Book of Revelation was originally given, how diligently have I read, studied, and applied it?

17. Do I realize that I need to pray for others that the Spirit will soften hearts & that it will not be my words that produce their decision to accept Jesus but the Spirit's direction?

18. Do I know enough about this book to even speak intelligently to others?

19.?

20. Do I proclaim that time is short & we need to be prepared?

21. Am I able to define "grace"? looked up: undeserved love God shows us in Christ, by which we are saved by nothing we do.

I need to become a student of the Word of God in order to apply it & proclaim it.

103

Revelation 22:6-21

Responding to God

Focus on what God is saying to you from this section's Scripture passages. Rewrite your responses below from each step 5 on the previous pages.

Revelation 22:6-9

Hope

Revelation 22:10-15

Revelation 22:16-21

Prayerfully review your responses. What will you do now? Write down today's date and what you will commit to do about what God has said.

Talk with God about your commitment. Pray for continued direction and a deeper relationship with God.

Revelation 22:6-21

VIDEO LISTENING SHEETS

Hope That Ignites Your Heart
Revelation 22:6-21

Jesus - "Heavenly Homemaker."

I. To Be Faithful to God's Word—Revelation 22:6-7

Hope that ignites your heart.

His Word is TRUE. — yesterday, today & tomorrow.
Do you believe it?
What are you going to do about it?

Real faith is backed by COMMITMENT.

Be faithful to His Word & obey it.

II. To Be Faithful to Worship—Revelation 22:8-9

DAILY LIGHT Devotional

How quickly John became unfocused — fell

Be careful to Keep your FOCUS on Jesus.

Deliberately decide How to Keep Your Focus!

early in the morning each day.

III. To Be Faithful to God's Work—Revelation 22:10-13

The Bible - from Gen - Rev — Says it all.

Nothing else to add, Nothing else needed.

Night is coming, What will you do while it is
still DAY.

Work for the prize that Jesus has for us

Live every moment as though I will be
face to face with Him in the next moment.

IV. To Be Faithful to Wash—Revelation 22:14-15

Isai "filty rags"

Jesus gives us His Perfect Robe of Righteousness
when we bow before the CROSS

Keep Short accounts with the Lord - everyday

Unconfessed Sin will disrupt the fellowship
& communication c̄ the Father.

Revelation 22:6-21

V. To Be Faithful to Witness—Revelation 22:16-17

We need to extend the invitation!

Do we notice those on the "outside"?

"Come" to the One who can meet all your needs.

VI. To Be Faithful to Warn—Revelation 22:18-19

... people who would add or subtract to God's Word.

VII. To Be Faithful to Watch—Revelation 22:20-21

for signs of return of Christ

Matt 24 "Signs of the times are like birth pains, ...
the worst tornadoes, earthquack, fires, etc.

Jesus is coming soon
Keep working but keep
With one eye watching for His arrival.

AFTERWORD

$\mathscr{A}$t the beginning of this workbook, a Bible study example was given using Mark 9 which describes the experience three disciples had as they witnessed the transfiguration of Jesus Christ. I wonder if Jesus had invited all of His disciples to draw aside and spend some time alone with Him, but only three out of the twelve accepted His invitation. However that may be, the three who spent time alone with Jesus received a fresh vision of His glory (see Mark 9:2-9), while those who did not faced massive confusion and problems which they had no power to solve (see Mark 9:14,17-18).

One of the problems the nine disciples faced was that of a father who brought to them his son, who was completely out of control. You can hear the father's anguished despair and frustration as he tells Jesus of his disappointment with the disciples' inability to help: "Teacher, I brought you my son ... I asked your disciples to drive out the spirit, but they could not" (Mark 9:17-18).

Later, when His disciples asked Jesus why they had no power to help the father or his son, He answered in a way that gives tremendous insight into our powerlessness to help others: " 'This kind can come forth by nothing, but by prayer and fasting.' " (Mark 9:29). In other words, our ability to help others is directly related to the time we spend in fasting—going without anything and everything in order to make the time to get alone with Jesus in prayer and the reading of His Word. Too often we put our work before our worship and end up with powerless, fruitless service.

Now that you have completed this workbook, make plans for the continued reading of God's Word. I pray God will richly bless you as you seek to maintain your vision of His glory, and in so doing, receive the power to make an impact in the lives of others.

MY COMMITMENT

Commit your way to the Lord;
trust in him.

Psalm 37:5

Just as Samuel set up a stone of remembrance saying, " 'Thus far has the Lord helped us' " (1 Sam. 7:12), use this time of commitment as a spiritual landmark in your journey of faith to remember God's faithfulness.

If God has spoken to you in this study and you have made a decision before Him, please indicate your decision here:

❐ I have been moved to accept Christ as my Savior.
❐ I have decided to renew and develop my relationship with God by spending time each day in prayer and in studying His Word.
❐ I choose to apply God's promise in _____ (Bible reference) to _____ (specific area/need in my life).
❐ Other commitments I wish to make:

_____

_____

Signed: _____

Date: _____

If you checked the first item above, share your decision with a Christian friend or minister. He or she will rejoice with you in your decision, pray with and for you, and provide you additional guidance. He or she will also help you become part of a church and join other believers in the body of Christ in worship and discipleship. If you checked any of the other items above, share your decision with a Christian friend. He or she will pray regularly for you and the specific decision you have made.

Consider removing this page from the book and keeping it as a "stone of remembrance." God bless you in your commitment.

You've done the study...
Now follow it up by reading the book!

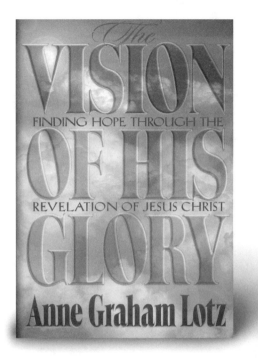

Continue your journey through Revelation. With skilled teaching, an inspiring sense of wonder, practical insight, and heart-touching parables, Anne Graham Lotz brings clarity and understanding to the glorious pageantry and awesome imagery of the book of Revelation. Sharing her passion for God's Word, she will lead you step by step through John's glorious, eyewitness account of God's plan for our future. Book: ISBN 0-8499-1216-4 Audiotape Set: ISBN 0-6330-3968-3

WORD PUBLISHING

Available at your local Christian Bookstore, or call toll free 800-233-1123.

God's Story

Finding Meaning for Your Life Through Knowing God

Anne Graham Lotz leads you through the first 11 chapters of Genesis, unlocking hidden meanings in the familiar stories of Creation, Adam and Eve, Noah and the ark, the Tower of Babel, and others. She thoughtfully illuminates each moment of Creation with inspiring insights and probing reflections to better reveal God, the Creator of us all. You'll thrill to the beauty and majesty and tenderness of God's personal involvement in creating the world, and you'll come to recognize the Creator's infinite power at work in your life as well. Book: ISBN 0-8499-1531-7

WORD PUBLISHING

Available at your local Christian bookstore, or call toll free 800-233-1123.

Daily Light for Every Day

Originally compiled many years ago by Samuel Bagster of London, England, *Daily Light* is an elegant leather-bound volume of morning and evening Bible readings for every day of the year, with an exclusive section of readings Anne Graham Lotz has selected for special occasions, suffering, struggles, success, salvation, secrets of life, and seasons of life. Anne says, "God has spoken to me more often through the verses in *Daily Light* than through any other book, except my Bible. Again and again, He has given me answers to questions, direction for ministry, comfort in distress, wisdom for decisions, and promises to cling to from the various selected Scriptures."

Black: ISBN 0-8499-5462-2
Tan: ISBN 0-8499-5464-9
Burgundy: ISBN 0-8499-5463-0
Forest green: ISBN 0-8499-5465-7

Available at your local Christian Bookstore, or call toll free 800-233-1123.

LIFEWAY RESOURCES

The following resources are available by **writing** LifeWay Church Resources Customer Service, MSN 113; 127 Ninth Avenue, North; Nashville, TN 37234-0113; **calling** 1-800-458-2772 (8:00 a.m.-5:00 p.m. CT, M-F, 24-hour voice mail ordering); **faxing** (615) 251-5933; **emailing** *customerservice@lifeway.com*; or **ordering online** at *www.lifeway.com*.

***Everyday Discipleship Series* provides easy-to-use, short-term studies for busy adults**
- *In God's Presence: Your Daily Guide to a Meaningful Prayer Life* by T.W. Hunt and Claude V. King (ISBN 0-8054-9900-8)
- *When God Speaks: How to Recognize God's Voice and Respond in Obedience* by Henry and Richard Blackaby (ISBN 0-8054-9822-2)
- *Living God's Word: Practical Lessons for Applying Scripture to Life* by Waylon Moore (ISBN 0-7673-2604-0)
- *The Kingdom Agenda: Experiencing God in Your Workplace* by Mike and Debi Rogers (ISBN 0-7673-3408-6)

In-depth small-group studies draw adults closer to God and His will for their lives

- *Experiencing God: Knowing and Doing the Will of God* by Henry T. Blackaby and Claude V. King (Member Book ISBN 0-8054-9954-7; Leader Guide ISBN 0-8054-9951-2)
- *The Mind of Christ* by T.W. Hunt and Claude V. King (Member Book ISBN 0-8054-9870-2; Leader Guide ISBN 0-8054-9869-9)
- *Disciple's Prayer Life: Walking in Fellowship with God* by T.W. Hunt and Catherine Walker (ISBN 0-7673-3494-9)

Bible studies that challenge and encourage women

- *To Live Is Christ: The Life and Ministry of Paul* by Beth Moore (Member Book ISBN 0-7673-3412-4; Leader Guide ISBN 0-7673-3411-6; Leader Kit with videotapes ISBN 0-7673-3402-7)
- *A Woman's Heart: God's Dwelling Place* by Beth Moore (Member Book ISBN 0-8054-9836-2; Leader Guide ISBN 0-7673-3401-9; Leader Kit with videotapes ISBN 0-8054-9826-5)
- *A Heart Like His: Seeking the Heart of God Through a Study of David* by Beth Moore (Member Book including leader guide ISBN 0-7673-2596-6; Leader Kit with videotapes ISBN 0-7673-2653-9)
- *Living Beyond Yourself: Exploring the Fruit of the Spirit* by Beth Moore (Member Book including leader guide ISBN 0-7673-9275-2)
- *Jesus, the One and Only* by Beth Moore (Member Book ISBN 0-76733275-X; Leader Guide ISBN 0-7673-3276-8; Leader Kit with videotapes ISBN 0-6330-0330-1)

Men's resources that promote spiritual growth

- *The Man God Uses: Moved from the Ordinary to the Extraordinary* by Henry and Tom Blackaby (Member Book ISBN 0-7673-3167-2; Leader Kit with videotape ISBN 0-7673-3183-4)
- *The Seven Seasons of a Man's Life* Series by Patrick Morley
  The Seasons of Reflection and Building (ISBN 0-8054-9788-9)
  The Seasons of Crisis and Renewal (ISBN 0-8054-9787-0)
  The Season of Rebuilding (ISBN 0-8054-9786-2)
  The Seasons of Suffering and Success (ISBN 0-8054-9785-4)
  Leader Kit ISBN 0-8054-9750-1
- *Men Leading the Charge* by Steve Farrar (Member Book ISBN 0-6?ˉ0764-1; Leader Kit with videotapes ISBN 0-6330-2949-1)

G R O U P   L E A D E R   G U I D E

The following Group Leader Guide includes:
- **Group Leader Ideas** (below)
- **Bible Study Workshop Plans** (pp. 118-119)
- **Group Session Plans** (pp. 120-125)

Group Leader Ideas

What?

A group study of *The Vision of His Glory* is appropriate for home and neighborhood groups, Bible study classes, accountability groups, discipleship and prayer groups, and one-on-one discipleship. The study will benefit adults of all ages. Promote the study by showing the promotional segment on tape one. Use the short version as an outreach tool on local TV and cable. You can order a broadcast quality version by calling (615) 251-5926.

When?

Meet at a time appropriate for your participants. Sessions can be conducted weekly, monthly, or any interval in between. Group sessions are designed for 90 minutes each, but allow the Holy Spirit to determine your schedule. For example, your group may decide to spend two group sessions on each seminar. Group plans in this section serve as a framework; your goal should be to meet the needs of your group.

Where?

Participants can meet at the church or in a home or business; anywhere that will accommodate a VCR/TV set-up and is conducive for discussion and prayer.

How?

Use the following group plans. As facilitator, you should:
- *Pray for group members before each session.*
- *Complete Bible study material for the session.*
- *Prepare material for the session; this includes securing video equipment to show the video presentations.*
- *Encourage group members.*
- *After each session, contact participants who were absent.*

Notes

BIBLE STUDY WORKSHOP

Notes

The Bible Study Workshop is a time of gathering and introducing group members, distributing and overviewing study materials, and participating in the workshop.

1. Begin on time. Participants introduce themselves by giving their names and one expectation they have of the study. Said another way, "Why are you here?"

2. Tell participants that prayer will be an important part of this study. Ask for prayer concerns and praises. Pray for the concerns shared and ask God to guide the group during the study.

3. Give each participant a copy of the workbook. Briefly overview the contents page and explain the progression of the study. Invite participants to turn to seminar 1 on page 17. Call attention to the two major sections in each seminar: individual study (p.18) and the video listening sheets (p. 30). Emphasize the importance of completing the Bible study material before each seminar session. Also review the "Study Note" in the box on page 7.

4. Explain the schedule your group will be following during the study. Also cover any other logistical issues such as when and where the group will meet, child care for those who need it, and so on.

5. Say, We will begin the study with a Bible Study Workshop. During the Bible Study Workshop, Anne Graham Lotz presents an approach that will help us know God in a personal relationship through His Word. The Bible study approach introduced in the workshop helps us communicate with God through the Bible.

6. Explain that this Bible study approach is introduced in detail through a video presentation. Invite participants to use the workshop section as a viewing guide to underline key thoughts and take additional notes as they participate in the workshop.

7. View the video presentation on the Bible Study Workshop (viewing time: 41 min.–does not include stopping the tape for the activities). Stop the tape as directed during the presentation. Allow the time recommended for participants to complete work. The following will be suggested during the presentation for each group activity.

First activity: What does the passage say?　　　　<u>10 minutes</u>
Completed individually

Second activity: What does the passage mean?　　　　<u>10 minutes</u>
Completed in small groups (three or four in a group)

Third activity: What does the passage mean to me?　　　<u>5 minutes</u>
Completed individually

Anne Graham Lotz debriefs each of these activities with her group. You will want to do the same before you restart the tape; then observe the examples and comments made on the videotape.

8. Inform participants about the audiotapes and how they can be used to review Anne's video presentation or to catch up with the group if they miss a session. You may want to have sets available for participants who want to use one.

9. Instruct participants to complete the Bible study material for the first seminar (begins on p. 18). Remind them to bring their workbooks, Bibles, and a pen or pencil with them to every group session. Announce the day, time, and place for the next session.

Notes

Seminar 1: Hope When You Are Depressed

Revelation 1:1-19

1. Begin on time. Make latecomers welcome with as little interruption as possible. Provide name tags during the first group session unless participants know each other well.

2. Say, Anne Graham Lotz says, "The Book of Revelation begins by clearly stating its theme: 'The revelation of Jesus Christ . . .' The word *revelation* literally means to 'unveil.' In the Book of Revelation, God uses prophecy to 'unveil' Jesus, enabling us to see Him in a unique way. And when we see Him clearly, we see a vision of His glory."

3. Say, As we begin our journey through the Book of Revelation, let's ask God to guide us so that we may experience the vision of His glory. Lead the group in prayer.

4. Before viewing the video of Seminar 1, review participants' responses to Steps 2, 3, 4, and 5 on each worksheet, pages 19-27. Focus on what God is saying to participants from this section's Scripture passages. Encourage participation from every group member without making anyone feel uncomfortable sharing.

5. View the video presentation of Seminar 1: Hope When You Are Depressed (viewing time: 50 min.). Encourage participants to open their Bibles to Revelation 1 and take careful notes during the presentation on the video listening sheets that begin on page 30. The presentation concludes with a music video of "Give Me Jesus."

6. Close by reading together the Scripture on page 17 that introduced the seminar: Colossians 1:27b and Jeremiah 29:11. Ask one of the participants to pray for the group for continued direction and a deeper relationship with God.

Seminar 2: Hope When You Are Deluded

Revelation 2:1-7; 3:1-22

1. Honor each participant's time commitment by starting on time. Read Ephesians 1:18a (p. 33) as a prayer to begin the session.

2. Say, In Revelation 2 and 3, God shines the light of His Word into the hearts of seven churches, revealing things that were not pleasing to Him and things the churches were not aware of based on their standards and perspectives. The churches seemed in danger of losing the vision of God's glory. We have focused on four of the seven churches in preparation for this seminar: the churches at Ephesus, Sardis, Philadelphia, and Laodicea. Let's view the seminar on "Hope When You Are Deluded."

3. Before viewing the video of Seminar 2, review participants' responses to Steps 2, 3, 4, and 5 on each worksheet, pages 34-41. Focus on what God is saying to participants as they studied and reflected on what He said to these four churches. Encourage participation from every group member without making anyone feel uncomfortable sharing.

4. View the video presentation of Seminar 2: Hope When You Are Deluded (viewing time: 54 min.). Encourage participants to open their Bibles to Revelation 2 and to take careful notes during the presentation on the video listening sheets that begin on page 44.

5. Close by reading together the Scripture on page 33 that introduced this seminar: Ephesians 1:18a. Pray for any concerns and needs facing group members as well as continued direction and a deeper relationship with God.

Notes

Seminar 3: Hope When You Are Discouraged

Revelation 4–5

1. As participants arrive, give each person an encouraging word, a firm handshake, a hug, or a pat on the back. Begin on time.

2. Say, When we realistically look at the condition of our world today, it is easy to become discouraged. In spite of the obedience, dependence, and service to God by Christians everywhere, things don't seem to be getting any better. That can leave us overwhelmed and discouraged. But the vision of God's glory that we see in Revelation 4 and 5 declares that Jesus is supreme as Lord and He is sufficient as Lamb.

3. Say, As we continue our journey through the Book of Revelation, let's ask God to guide us so that we may experience hope when we are discouraged. Lead the group in prayer.

4. Before viewing the video of Seminar 3, review participants' responses to Steps 2, 3, 4, and 5 on each worksheet, pages 50-59. Focus on what God is saying to participants from this section's Scripture passages. Encourage participation from every group member without making anyone feel uncomfortable sharing.

5. View the video presentation of Seminar 3: Hope When You Are Discouraged (viewing time: 52 min.). Encourage participants to open their Bibles to Revelation 4 and take careful notes during the presentation on the video listening sheets that begin on page 62.

6. Close by reading together the Scriptures on page 49 that introduced the seminar: Psalm 39:7; 71:14. Ask two or three participants to voice prayers of encouragement for the group during times of discouragement.

Notes

Seminar 4: Hope When You Are Distressed

Revelation 6–19

1. Begin on time. Ask, "What current event in our world causes you to say, 'It just isn't fair! It's not right! How can they get by with that?' " Allow several participants to respond.

2. Say, Anne Graham Lotz says, "Like the piercing rays of the sun penetrating through dark storm clouds, the vision of God's glory penetrates our distress over evil actions and evil alliances, setting us free to place our hope in the One alone who is absolutely just and merciful." This week we have studied a portion of the Book of Revelation that brings hope to our distress. Lead the group in prayer.

3. Before viewing the video of Seminar 4, review participants' responses to Steps 2, 3, 4, and 5 on each worksheet, pages 68-75. Focus on what God is saying to participants from this section's Scripture passages. Encourage participation from every group member without making anyone feel uncomfortable sharing.

4. View the video presentation of Seminar 4: Hope When You Are Distressed (viewing time: 55 min.). Encourage participants to open their Bibles to Revelation 6 and take careful notes during the presentation on the video listening sheets that begin on page 78.

5. Close by reading together the Scripture on page 67 that introduced the seminar: Psalm 33:18-19 and Psalm 42:5. Ask several participants to offer prayers of praise for the hope we have as Christians that one day Jesus Christ will appear to rescue, to rule, and to reign on this earth.

Notes

Seminar 5: Hope When You Are Defeated

Revelation 21

1. Write the word *home* on a large piece of paper and hang it in a prominent place so participants can see it when they enter.

2. Begin the session with a time of prayer for concerns and praises of group members.

3. Ask, What does the word *home* mean to you? Allow several to answer. List their answers on the piece of paper as they are shared. Answers might include love, acceptance, security, comfort; a place where I can find answers, take my burdens, get my needs met.

4. Say, *Home* means many things to many people. No matter how positive our view of home is, it will not compare to the heavenly home Jesus has promised those who love Him. Revelation 21 provides us a glimpse of our heavenly home.

5. Before viewing the video of Seminar 5, review participants' responses to Steps 2, 3, 4, and 5 on each worksheet, pages 84-91. Focus on what God is saying to participants from this section's Scripture passages. Encourage participation from every group member without making anyone feel uncomfortable sharing.

6. View the video presentation of Seminar 5: Hope When You Are Defeated (viewing time: 50 min.). Encourage participants to open their Bibles to Revelation 21 and take careful notes during the presentation on the video listening sheets that begin on page 94. Be sensitive to God's Holy Spirit moving in the lives of members in your group. Allow time for reflection and commitment during the music video presentation and before you move to step 6.

7. Read together 1 Corinthians 15:19 on page 83. Say, The vision of God's glory gives us hope because it reveals that this world is not our home, death does not have the final word, and one day our faith will become sight and we will see the gates of Heaven open and hear our Lord say, "Welcome home." Close with prayer.

Seminar 6: Hope That Ignites Your Heart

Revelation 22:6-21

1. Begin on time. Ask participants to share briefly examples from their past when they experienced true faithfulness from a friend or family member. Then ask the group to list characteristics of someone who is faithful. List these on a large sheet of paper.

2. Say, Anne Graham Lotz says, "The vision of His glory concludes with a challenge to us to experience the difference hope does make today. We are challenged not to place our hope in things of this world but to keep our focus on the rising Son in every aspect of our lives. The vision of His glory ignites our hearts with passionate anticipation, challenging us to live faithfully every day, every hour, every moment in the light of the imminent return of the One who alone is worthy as the only Hope of the world!"

3. Before viewing the video of Seminar 6, review participants' responses to Steps 2, 3, 4, and 5 on each worksheet, pages 99-103. Focus on what God is saying to participants from this section's Scripture passages. Encourage participation from every group member without making anyone feel uncomfortable sharing.

4. View the video presentation of Seminar 6: Hope That Ignites Your Heart (viewing time: 58 min.). Encourage participants to open their Bibles to Revelation 22 and take careful notes during the presentation on the video listening sheets that begin on page 106.

5. Invite participants to turn to page 111, My Commitment. Say, At the end of the following video segment during the music, reflect on any significant response you have made in this study. Show Anne's closing comments and the music segment that follows the seminar presentation (viewing time: 6 min.). After the video, ask those who will to share their commitments. Affirm those who share, and pledge your continued love and support in the days ahead.

6. Close with prayer. Invite participants to pray verbally for each other for continued direction and a deeper relationship with God.

CHRISTIAN GROWTH STUDY PLAN

Preparing Christians to Serve

the **Christian Growth Study Plan (formerly
 urch Study Course)**, this book *The Vision of
 s Glory* is a resource for course credit in the
 bject area PERSONAL LIFE of the Christian
 owth category of diploma plans. To receive
 edit, read the book, complete the learning activ-
 es, show your work to your pastor, a staff
 ember or church leader, then complete the
 llowing information. This page may be
 plicated. Send the completed page to:

**Christian Growth Study Plan
127 Ninth Avenue, North, MSN 117
Nashville, TN 37234-0117
FAX: (615)251-5067**

For information about the Christian Growth Study
Plan, refer to the current Christian Growth Study
Plan Catalog. Your church office may have a copy.
If not, request a free copy from the Christian
Growth Study Plan office (615/251-2525).

The Vision of His Glory
COURSE NUMBER: CG- 0475

PARTICIPANT INFORMATION

Social Security Number (USA ONLY)	Personal CGSP Number*	Date of Birth (MONTH, DAY, YEAR)

Name (First, Middle, Last)		Home Phone
☐ Mr. ☐ Miss		
☐ Mrs. ☐		

Address (Street, Route, or P.O. Box)	City, State, or Province	Zip/Postal Code

CHURCH INFORMATION

Church Name

Address (Street, Route, or P.O. Box)	City, State, or Province	Zip/Postal Code

CHANGE REQUEST ONLY

☐ Former Name

☐ Former Address	City, State, or Province	Zip/Postal Code

☐ Former Church	City, State, or Province	Zip/Postal Code

Signature of Pastor, Conference Leader, or Other Church Leader	Date

*New participants are requested but not required to give SS# and date of birth. Existing participants, please give CGSP# when using SS# for the first time.
  Thereafter, only one ID# is required. **Mail to:** Christian Growth Study Plan, 127 Ninth Ave., North, Nashville, TN 37234-0117. Fax: (615)251-5067